Jesus & K

The Hidden Treasure

Paul A. Westerman

www.pawesterman.com

THANK YOU

In writing this book I have received the encouragement and guidance of Rabbi Meir Yeshurun the head of the London Kabbalah Centre and his predecessor Marcus Weston. I have also benefited from the not inconsiderable enthusiasm and constructive criticism from Gladys Obadiah a founding Trustee of the London Kabbalah Centre.

With each of them I have engaged in many frank discussions but always with a loving heart and good wishes. Thank you.

I also give thanks to the many loving and highly spiritual clergy, monks and academics it has been my privilege to meet over many years of enquiry and searching.

But this book would not have been possible without the particular assistance of my youngest son, my family and friends who have supported me for many years and in many ways. Thank you all.

Whilst it is appropriate that I should give all of these people the credit they deserve it is of course right that I accept that any errors in what I have written are entirely my responsibility. Notwithstanding, I hope that you receive at least as much pleasure in reading this book as I have had in writing it.

Paul A. Westerman

London

2017

Contents

Introduction

In the Courts of England and Wales, the Royal Coat of Arms hangs behind and above the Judges head, on which the words 'Dieu et mon droit' are inscribed. There is some disagreement as to the precise interpretation but the phrase is generally understood to mean 'God and my right'. It is almost certainly a reference to a monarch's appointment by God – the divine right of a king or queen to rule, to make laws, to judge them and enforce them. The divine right of kings is a central theme in the 'history' plays of Shakespeare. Only a divinely appointed and anointed king or queen could claim legitimacy and succession to rule.

The coronation of the King or Queen of the United Kingdom (and other territories) is performed in a church by the clergy. It is really in the nature of a religious service.

Although not officially part of the inauguration ceremony as prescribed by the United States Constitution, in practice the President of the United States when being inaugurated swears an oath which concludes with the words 'So help me God'. The word 'inauguration' is derived from Latin words that have their root in the sacred. The inauguration of the President of the United States of America is a sacred ceremony.

The recognition of 'something' more powerful by the most powerful people on earth reaches back throughout human history. Even today, when a large number of people are turning away from organised religion, especially in what is described as 'the West', the belief in God or a Creator is held by all but a relative small percentage of the population. The issue for people does not seem so much to be about believing in a Creator as believing in the Creator or 'God' that is presented to them by the major religions. This is especially true in the Christian and Jewish religions. The majority of the followers 'believe' in 'God' but only a very small minority regularly attend church or synagogue.

When we reflect on human history and the things that have been said and done purportedly in the name of 'God', it is not surprising that we are perplexed and dismayed by the notion of a God that apparently is the Creator of all things – and yet seems to allow, if not condone, the infliction of such utter misery and suffering on so many.

Forty years ago in the crisp December air just outside my local Parish Church, following a delightful Christmas Eve service, the question that was put to me was this:

'If there is a God, why is there so much evil in the world?'

The implication being, that God is responsible for the evil that exists in the world. It took me a while to work out the answer but I believe that it is this.

- Evil is the total absence of God.
- God is the total absence of evil.
- God created the world including the potential for good and evil – and everything in between.
- We have an opportunity in every minute of every day to choose good.

Actually, when you think about it, there aren't that many evil people in the world. When we talk of evil in the world we are usually referring to the words and/or actions of a small number of people. But that small minority can impact on a very large number of people – precisely because those people are more good than evil.

As shown in the table below, I would say that most human behaviour falls in the middle zone and those at the outer extremes at both ends being very much the exceptions.

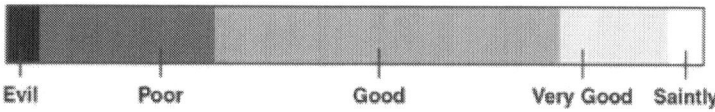

| Evil | Poor | Good | Very Good | Saintly |

The question then arises - 'why' were we given a choice to choose between good and evil? Since whom in their right mind would choose evil? I will come to that later.

But perhaps a fundamental question is 'why' we exist at all to be in a position to make a choice? That is the hardest question to answer. But I try to do so in the final chapter.

At the heart of this book is the relationship we have with the 'Creator' or the 'Source of all things' – seen and unseen. Christians refer to that 'Creator' as God. Jews have an ineffable name that they will not utter and Kabbalists have at least 72 names to describe that 'thing' that brought creation into being and maintains its existence.

This book seeks to explain what it is like to be connected to God, where and how to find that connection, and how a Jewish Rabbi – Yeshua (the person we now know by the name Jesus - the Christ) - taught about it – and only it – with an authority that almost certainly has its source in the ancient secret and esoteric wisdom of what we now know as Kabbalah.

Yeshua was not a Christian.

Yeshua was a Jewish Rabbi – a spiritual teacher. If we are to believe at least some of what is written in the Christian's New Testament, Yeshua taught from the Torah in numerous synagogues and on many occasions in the Temple in Jerusalem. He was repeatedly consulted and questioned by other Rabbis and other Jewish religious people.

The Table below is illustrative of this point:

	Matthew	Mark	Luke
Synagogue(s)	4:23, 9:35, 13:54	1:21, 3:1, 6:2	4:15, 4:16, 4:33, 4:44, 6:6, 13:10
Temple	21:12, 21:23	11:15, 11:27, 12:35	19:45, 19:47, 20:1, 21:37
Sadducees/Pharisees, Scribes, Seeking out	8:19, 9:18, 12:2, 12:38, 15:1, 16:1, 19:3, 21:12, 21:14, 21:23, 21:45, 22:15, 22:23, 22:34, 24:1	2:16, 2:23, 3:22, 5:22, 7:1, 8:11, 10:2, 12:13, 12:18, 12:28. 12:41	5:17, 5:30, 6:6-7, 7:36, 10:25, 11:37, 11:45, 13:31, 14:1, 17:20, 18:18, 20:1 20:20, 20:27

To his contemporaries, he would have been known as Rabbi Yeshua. But he was more than a Rabbi – he was a prodigy.

As I shall show, he was almost certainly a Kabbalist - versed in the secret knowledge that underpin the coded messages to be found in the Torah and the Hebrew Bible – the Old Testament.

Until now I have repeatedly used the name Yeshua to emphasise the Jewishness of the person we call Jesus. But from now on I shall refer to him simply as, Jesus.

Although Kabbalah is more widely heard of now, not least because of some of its famous adherents - it was not always that way. It is thanks to the work of Rabbi Philip Berg, his family (wife Karen, sons Yehudi and Michael) and many other dedicated people at the Kabbalah Centre created in the 1960s. What was formerly only revealed to a very select few Jewish Rabbis, is available to everyone and not just people who follow Judaism. It is now accessible to anyone of any faith (or none) should they chose to enquire.

Kabbalah has its source in Judaism. But of course, the original Christian Church - The Holy Roman Catholic Church – also has its roots in Judaism. The Catholic Church is fully aware of Kabbalah. Both it and The Anglican Church have had a 2000 years connection and relationship with it. They have both tried to keep it a secret.

For instance, have you ever noticed that the Pope wears a Jewish Kippah on his head? Is that a coincidence?

The paintings by Michelangelo (whose close friend was a leading Kabbalist) in the Sistine Chapel in the Vatican in Rome, contain numerous Kabbalah symbols. Is this a coincidence too?

Sir Isaac Newton the famous physicist, mathematician and astronomer was an ordained Anglican priest. He studied Kabbalah and owned a copy of one of its most famous texts – the Zohar. His copy of the Zohar is still held at Trinity College Cambridge and can upon request be inspected there.

The awareness of and connection between Jesus and Kabbalah may not be as well known amongst Christians as it is amongst Kabbalists, but that is now changing – and this book is the first to reveal some of the hidden connections between the teachings of Jesus as found in the Synoptic Gospels and the teachings of Kabbalah.

Although he has often been referred to as Jesus of Nazareth, we cannot know with absolute certainty that this was his place of birth or where he grew up. The Synoptic Gospels and other parts of the New Testament may have caused confusion in variously alluding to Jesus as being an inhabitant of Nazareth (a small village near to the Sea of Galilee in Israel) and being a Nazarite (or Nazarene) – a member of a religious sect of Judaism.

In Numbers 6:1 of the Torah (Old Testament) a Nazarite is someone who is 'consecrated' or 'separated' by a particular set of vows. Samson [Judges 13:5] is specifically referred to as a Nazarite.

Even so, there is considerable evidence to establish that Jesus taught and travelled throughout a portion of his adult life in, around and even on the Sea of Galilee in Northern Israel.

As any Kabbalist will confirm, Rabbi Shimon bar Yochai - one of Kabbalah's most famous teachers was also born in Galilee - around 40 AD. Like Jesus – Rabbi Shimon was a Jewish Rabbi and like Jesus his everyday language was Aramaic. The book that that Kabbalists say that Rabbi Shimon wrote (or rather revealed) is called the Zohar, which is written in Aramaic. There are certainly many interesting connections to discuss here. Indeed, as I shall show, there is evidence that Kabbalah reveals itself as being at the core of Jesus' teaching – a teaching so simple and yet so profound. A core teaching that seems to have been made unnecessarily complicated; hidden under layers of misunderstanding, mistranslation and distortion.

Once properly understood, the core teaching of Jesus points to the ultimate source of all power and happiness – and he tells us that it is within our reach to enjoy it – now – and be rid of evil. This source, the path to that source and the nature of the source may have been hidden by organised Christian and Judaic religion quite unwittingly, but now it is time to lift the veil and reveal it for everyone's benefit – especially yours.

The First Precept as stated in 'The Zohar' – a foundational Kabbalist text is:

"To be in awe of God – is the beginning of wisdom and the gateway through which one enters into Faith"

Below is an extract of this precept from The Zohar in the original Aramaic together with a translation into English. I also provide a transliteration and strongly urge you to read these words aloud.

"(A) The first precept:

> This is the first step in developing a true connection and attachment to the Light of the Creator. To violate this particular precept is to transgress all the precepts of the Torah.

Original Aramaic

189. בְּרֵאשִׁית בָּרָא אֱלֹהִים. הֲדָא הִיא פִּקּוּדָא קַדְמָאָה דְכֹלָּא וְאִקְרֵי פִּקּוּדָא דָא יִרְאַת ה', דְּאִקְרֵי רֵאשִׁית, דִּכְתִיב רֵאשִׁית חָכְמָה יִרְאַת ה'. יִרְאַת ה' רֵאשִׁית דַּעַת. בְּגִין דְּמִלָּה דָא רֵאשִׁית אִקְרֵי, וְדָא אִיהִי תַּרְעָא לְעָאלָא גּוֹ מְהֵימְנוּתָא, וְעַל פִּקּוּדָא דָא אִתְקַיַּים כָּל עָלְמָא.

Transliteration*

189. בְּרֵאשִׁית BERESHEET בָּרָא BARA אֱלֹהִים ELOHIM

. הָדָא HADA הִיא HEE פִּקּוּדָא PIKUDA קַדְמָאָה

KADAMAAH דְּכֹלָּא DEKOLA וְאִקְרֵי VEIKREI פִּקּוּדָא

PIKUDA דָּא DA יִרְאַת YIRAT ה' HASHEM, דְּאִקְרֵי

DEIKREI רֵאשִׁית RESHEET, דִּכְתִיב DIKHTIV רֵאשִׁית

RESHEET חָכְמָה KHOCHMA יִרְאַת YIRAT ה' HASHEM.

יִרְאַת YIRAT ה' HASHEM רֵאשִׁית RESHEERT דַּעַת

DAAT. בְּגִין BEGIN דְּמִלָּה DEMILAH דָּא DA רֵאשִׁית

RESHEET אִקְרֵי IKREI, וְדָא VEDA אִיהִי IHEE תַּרְעָא

TARA לְעֵאלָּא LEALA גּוֹ GO מְהֵימְנוּתָא MEHEMANUTA,

וְעַל VEAL פִּקּוּדָא PIKUDA דָּא DA

אִתְקַיַּים ITKAYEM כָּל KOL עָלְמָא ALMA.

*Read from right to left so here start with 'Beresheet, Bara, Elohim…Alma'].

Translation

189. "In the beginning. Elohim created" (Beresheet 1:1). This is the first and foremost precept of all. And this precept is called "the fear of the Hashem," which is called the "beginning." As it is written, "The Fear of Hashem is the beginning of wisdom" (Tehilim 111:10); "The fear of Hashem is the beginning of knowledge" (Mishlei 1:7). Because this fear (or awe) is called a beginning. And it is the gateway through which one enters into Faith. So based on this precept, the whole world is able to exist"

[The Zohar - Volume 1 – Prologue – Page 114]

What is remarkable for me and I hope to all of you non-Kabbalists, is that what is offered here is the opportunity to speak in Aramaic. When the transliteration is uttered aloud, we are speaking in the very language that Jesus spoke.

Of course, his pronunciation was better than ours (!) – but just pause to think about it.

In uttering the words above from Paragraph 189 (Beresheet, Bara, Elohim etc) you are speaking and understanding for the first time the language that Jesus spoke. Amazing.

As we shall see, the means to a happy and fulfilling life by forming a direct relationship with the Creator - is at the very heart of the core teaching of Jesus.

Chapter 1 –
Happiness

None of us desire unhappiness.

When we come to think about it, regardless of race, sex, age, culture, religion or no religion; deep down, deep within us, we all desire the same thing.

What is it that we desire? It is lasting and deep happiness. Not just 'happiness' but deep and lasting happiness - a happiness that would be like heaven on earth.

I know you are thinking 'no', what I really want is more money'.

Clearly money is not intrinsically 'happy'. It is the 'things' that you can acquire using money that we think will provide happiness. Having more money is about having more things and therefore more happiness. That is a logical conclusion but it does not seem to work like that.

We are all of us conditioned to believe that if we have more money, we can buy more things; therefore, we should work harder to get more money.

Work = Money

Money = Happiness.

Therefore:

More Work = More Money

More Money = More Happiness

But think about that. If simply having lots of money made people deeply and lastingly happy, then people with more money than you would be incrementally happier than you. However, they are not. Likewise, people who have less money than you would be unhappier than you. But they are not either – at least not all of them. It would seem that deep and lasting happiness, a happiness that would be like heaven on earth, cannot be bought.

Indeed, on deeper reflection, you realise that the idea of having some money – or more money - is about banishing the fear of not having enough or any money. In other words, having more money provides some relief from fear, but that is not quite the same as happiness, let alone deep and lasting happiness.

The truth is that money does not make anyone happy – or if it does – it is not for long.

Moreover, any 'thing' that you acquire does not seem to provide happiness that lasts for long. The world in which most of us live is based on things not lasting either because they wear out or because they fall out of fashion.

So we look for happiness in what is new – whether that is a person or an object. We move onto the next new thing, then the next new thing and so on. This is part of a delusion that forms part of our daily lives.

Perhaps therefore, in looking for happiness, we are looking in the wrong place, seeking in the wrong direction what it is or where it is that happiness is found. Of course, in the world in which we live, money is necessary and useful - and it is usually better to have some money than no money at all. But of itself, it clearly does not provide or buy deep and lasting happiness.

This book has as its source in deep and lasting happiness, and it is written to share with you where and how you might find it. Happiness; especially a deep and lasting one, is a treasure, a gem that seems to be hidden from us. If you want to find it, you will if you work at it – and when you do find it – like me, you will want for nothing else. You will also want to share it with everyone you meet. In fact, you will have no choice. You will radiate happiness without even trying to do so.

Sometimes we experience some fleeting happiness – but very rarely if at all is it a deep and lasting happiness. As a matter of fact, happiness of the deep and lasting kind is so elusive - that most of us have come to the conclusion that such a happiness is not only scarce – but doesn't actually exist. But it does exist! If only you made half the effort to find it as you do to earn money – I guarantee that you will find it.

Many believe that sustained happiness is an impossibility. We have learned or been brainwashed to accept that happiness is and can only be at best fleeting and shallow. I do not believe that to be the case. However, I believe that it is easier to find once you know where to look. But it still requires effort.

Deep and lasting happiness is not just available to you, finding it and keeping it is why you were born. The problem is that we have been taught to search for happiness in the wrong place. As a result, our efforts have been misguided and misplaced. A waste of time.

As humans, almost without exception, we have become conditioned by each of our different societies to seek happiness in different things and different ways – but rarely in the right things or in the right way.

First of all in most societies especially in 'the West' we seek happiness in 'things' whether they are objects, people, ideologies, religion or events.

What is clear is that we are not taught or conditioned to look for happiness in the one and only place that it can be found. It is hidden from us. If we do look in or towards that place, the influence of everyday life comes rushing in and takes up most if not all the space we had created for our search.

If we truly wish to find deep and lasting happiness, a happiness that is like heaven here on earth, these are the things that we need to do:

- Acknowledge the desire to be happy.
- Review and decide what it is that makes us happy without having to spend any money – or at least very little money.
- Shift our focus from where we currently look for happiness.
- Focus on where we know happiness can be found.
- Commit our energies primarily (not exclusively) towards securing happiness in the new direction.

In summary:

- Decide where deep and lasting happiness is to be found and make that our new and primary target.
- Direct our energies towards the new target.

This teaching is something that has been available for thousands of years, but for a very long time has been misunderstood, forgotten or hidden.

I am going to reveal to you in this Book:

- What deep and lasting happiness is; and
- Where you can find it; and
- How to achieve it: and
- How Jesus' core message and Kabbalah point to the same source of happiness.

This is not a religious book. It is a spiritual book. It is a book that is about helping you find what you have either consciously or subconsciously been searching for all your life.

As will become apparent later, I use the word 'God' as a convenient way of expressing that 'thing' that might also be called;

1. The Creator
2. The Light
3. Allah
4. The Uncaused Cause
5. The Source
6. The Tao (pronounced Dow)
7. The One
8. Existence
9. YHWH

Please feel free to substitute the word God (which anyway is a pagan word) with any of the above or any other epithet that you prefer. Whatever works for you is fine. The word does not matter so long as it is pointing to the same 'thing'. It is simply a tool to reach a better understanding – and ultimately a 'sensing' of the presence of that which cannot be known nor fully described.

Personally, I prefer the word 'Creator' since it points more accurately to what might be said to be one of the most important features of the source of all things. But for the main part in this book I have used the word 'God', as it is that word that is more often found in the source materials of Christianity and Kabbalah.

For me, 'God' is beyond human knowing in the sense of knowing by any of our five senses and mind. At best, we can come to understand or sense by rational thought;

- that there was something before the moment of creation (what nowadays scientists call the 'big bang'), that that brought the big bang into being.

- that something had within it everything that we now know as the Universe – and more – indeed everything.

- that something isn't really some 'thing' - but in human terms we can describe 'it', 'him', or her' as having qualities which from a human perspective we cannot understand, namely, 'it' is infinite and beyond time.

Describing God as the Creator or as the Uncaused Cause serves as a reminder of what God is not. God is;

- Not - caused by anything else – there is no thing before or beyond God.
- Not - Human (or vegetable or mineral, organic/inorganic matter)
- Not - Some 'thing' (e.g. energy, material)
- Not - a (no) 'thing' – since that is the opposite of some 'thing'. [You cannot have no thing as a concept without some thing – and since God clearly isn't some thing but rather 'every thing' which includes 'some thing' and 'no thing']

- Not - Limited in time or space – is not finite in time and space.

In short, God or 'it' is for the main part a complete mystery. The reason for this is that so far as we know 'some thing', i.e. the Universe, came out of 'no thing' (as we understand that concept) – and that – from a human perspective is not possible. But it must be possible- because it happened. In fact, Creation came from everything – since God is the source of all things – and that is everything. God is therefore everything.

From our human perspective, absolutely everything that has come into existence has been brought into existence by something else. Science at every level can explain a great deal about the things in the Universe and even about the big bang. Science can explain by a process of deduction and reductionism that the big bang took place. I agree that it did.

But - what caused the so-called 'big bang' and all the energy and material within it to come into being? Indeed, what caused the thing, that caused the thing, that caused the 'big bang' to come into being? And so on.

The diagram overleaf seeks to illustrate this point.

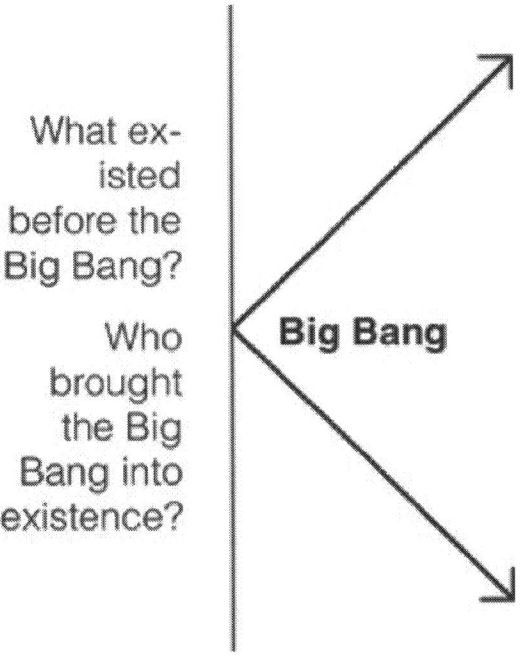

When science explains the origin of the Universe it is using concepts that have in-built limitations of experiment, observation, understanding and explanations namely:

Time
Space
Matter/Energy

Our understanding of anything and everything is limited by the human condition – by being human. Being human is to be limited in time, space and physicality – or form/energy.

Science can only observe what it can measure – and it cannot measure things that are outside of Time, Space and Energy.

Thus - Science cannot explain how the 'big bang' came into being in the first place. It cannot explain how something came out of 'nothing'. Believe me – it cannot and it does not even try to. Such concepts are beyond the boundaries of the laws of physics. Science can take us back to a certain point in time and space – and that is it. But science by its own laws knows that there is something beyond – that it cannot explain.

Yet – we do know this - and it and its importance to us is something that has been forgotten by most of us and for a very long time.

"The Universe was created by or out of something and <u>we</u> owe our very existence to that 'something'."

The fact that the Universe exists, that you and I exist, that anything exists, is not just a mystery in terms of how we came to exist – which is what science tries to understand.

"Indeed, the greatest mystery of all is <u>'why'</u> anything exists at all."

I have come to understand that focusing our energies in considering how and why we exist is how and where we discover deep and lasting happiness.

In doing so, we look closer at all creation to see with awe and wonder and astonishment the incredible complexity and vastness of everything that exists – from the very small to the very large – and everything in between - even and especially you and I.

When Jesus and Kabbalah talk about the First of all Commandments, this is what they are referring to:

"The Lord is our God. The Lord is alone. You shall love the Lord your God with all your heart, and with all your soul, and with all your might"

[Deuteronomy 6:4-5]

Understanding what it means to love God - the Creator of all things - so fully and who or what we mean when we say God, is in fact at the very heart of what Jesus and Kabbalah teach – and what this book is about.

This book explains the relevance of these teachings today and how powerful they will be when properly understood, in providing you with deep and lasting happiness.

I am going to explain the following (and remember please feel free to change the word God to something you feel more comfortable with):

- What it means to love God.

- Why loving God in the sense that I am going to explain leads to deep and lasting happiness – whether you are rich, poor, or anything in between.

- How your life will improve by following this one simple guide.

- How loving your neighbour will lead to and produce the first of all commandments.

- How Jesus and Kabbalah have been pointing to these truths; why they have been hidden and why they are being made known now.

If you want to know and experience deep and lasting happiness - then please read on.

Who would you invite to Tea?

If there were one person that you would like to sit down and talk to from any period of history including today, who would that be? Who would be your special guest at a dinner party or for tea? Who would you love to sit down and talk to about their life and vice versa? If you had a limited amount of time with that person, what would be the burning questions that you would ask?

For me there is only one person and that is Jesus.

A very close second if not equal first would be Moses. But then there is Rav Shimon bar Yochai, Siddhartha Gautama (the Buddha), or the Prophet Mohammad. It would be difficult to choose. Each of them has had and continues to have a profound impact upon the world. Not all of it good.

It would be interesting to also pose the same question to each of them. Who would they choose to have a tête-a-tête with?

However, I would choose Jesus who I have studied most and whose words and deeds I have reflected upon for almost my entire life. I do of course have some acquaintance with the others mentioned above - but not so much as with Jesus.

Think of the questions you might ask? What do you think Jesus would make of the religion and all that has been done and is still being done ostensibly in his name – Christ, Christian, Christianity?

Would he laugh or cry?

Once I had got over the shock of what he actually looked like, the colour of his eyes, his hair, beard, teeth, hands, feet (with sandals of course) his physical height, weight and the colour of his skin, here are the ten questions that I would love to ask Jesus?

1. Have you read the New Testament?
2. Is what is written about you accurate and true?

3. Who was your teacher?
4. What did you really mean when you talk about Metanoia?
5. Was your message for all or just Jews?
6. Is your core message concerning the Kingdom the same today as 2000 years ago?
7. What would you advise Christians today?
8. Were you really resurrected spiritually or physically or both?
9. Did you really claim to be 'the Messiah'?
10. What is life after death like?

The answers would no doubt give rise to yet further questions and some of them more mundane.

What questions would you ask your special guest?

Equally interesting would be to know what questions your special guest might ask you? How would you feel in his/her presence? Over awed? Humbled? Disappointed?

At one point many years ago, I was asked by the Catholic Church to help in teaching 'new recruits' and 'converts' about the fundamental 'beliefs' and precepts of the Catholic Church - that of course included the teachings of Jesus.

Ironically, by the time of this invitation I had come to understand that what I was being asked to teach was as much about the beliefs of the Catholic Church's man-made rules, than the essential, inspiring, urgent core message of its 'inspirer' – Jesus. In the circumstances I declined the invitation and ceased to be a practising Catholic. Instead I followed the advice that Jesus reportedly gave in order to find the answers to the many questions I still had;

"Whenever you pray, go into your room and shut the door and pray to your Father who is in secret"

and whilst there

"Seek and you will find"

[Matthew 7:7]

What was it that I was seeking? I have little doubt that it was not too dissimilar from what you and everyone else is seeking.

What is that? It is the movement away from the internal anxiety, suffering and unhappiness I seemed to be constantly experiencing – and instead moving toward lasting and deep happiness.

Religion, Churches, Synagogues, Mosques, Chapels, are not our ultimate source of lasting happiness. They are man-made (though often divinely inspired) and are simply signposts – a means to an end – not the end itself.

We should not go to Church or Synagogue to worship the institution, its rules or the people that 'preach' in it.

26

At best, the institutions are the custodians of the teaching or message from which it owes its existence.

As I will confirm in this book, Jesus was a Rabbi - a teacher. What he had to say and meant is far more important than the organisation that developed after his preaching had stopped. This is true of Judaism also. What God said and meant through the Three Patriarchs (Abraham, Isaac and Jacob), Noah, Moses, David and the Torah is more important than the 'religion' that grew around that – much of which is man-created anyway.

That having been said, Christians and Jews should be (and no doubt are) grateful that Christian Churches and Synagogues exist. They have helped to preserve over two thousand years (and more) the core documents (Torah/New Testament/Zohar and tradition) that contain the teachings of the person that forms the source of their existence.

The human communities and physical buildings have kept alive at least the possibility of re-discovering what Jesus and the Torah originally taught.

I hope that I can reveal to you that once the 'real' message of Jesus (the Jewish Rabbi) is understood; once the shrouds of man made errors and distortion have been removed and the veil of time lifted - the essential teaching of Jesus is directly linked to Moses and is as relevant today as it was 2000 years ago – and before that.

It is noted several times in the New Testament that Jesus spoke as though he had a unique wisdom and authority.

An examination of the synoptic Gospels of Matthew, Mark and Luke point to Jesus being aware of and teaching the esoteric (hidden) aspect of Judaism, now known as 'Kabbalah'.

It is recognised within Orthodox Judaism that Kabbalah has been part of Judaism since the time of Adam, Abraham, Moses, the Ten Commandments – and possibly before.

Topics that Jesus is repeatedly reported as teaching bear a remarkable resemblance to Kabbalah's position on;

- The Kingdom of God or Heaven
- Loving your neighbour
- Faith
- Repentance
- Resurrection

I will explain how the sayings of Jesus appear to be directly related to Kabbalah and may account for the 'wisdom' and 'authority' that is so frequently alluded to in the Synoptic Gospels. But more than this – I will reveal how once properly understood, the simple core message of Jesus and its parallels in Kabbalah - will give you the power to find deep and lasting happiness – what Jesus would describe as Heaven – yes Heaven - here on Earth for you.

Chapter 2 –
The Hidden Treasure

We are faced each day with choices as to where we should apply our energies in the pursuit of happiness.

In effect, we are making a decision as to what we consider to be of most value to us – what we treasure.

The table below is illustrative of some of these decisions.

Table of choices (Treasure Chest)

Material   **Spiritual**

Material	Spiritual
Money	Connecting to God/Creator
Winning	Peace of mind
Big House	Sharing your love, time and resources with your family
Nice car	Sharing your love, time, resources with friends/others
Respect of others	Receiving the love of others
Nice clothes	Good Health
Nice holidays	An absence of fear

Career	Self Awareness
Smartphone	Wisdom

Going back to your special guest from Chapter 1. If you asked them what they would recommend you to seek to fulfil your desire for deep and lasting happiness – which of the above do you think they would recommend? The question is 'where are your energies best served in the pursuit of happiness?'

What would you recommend to your wife, husband, partner, son, daughter or friend?

In case there is any misunderstanding, I am not saying that it is not good and pleasurable to have any and all of the things listed in the left column. I am simply inviting you to consider to what - after pausing and thinking about it; if given a choice – would most of your energies be directed. Maybe not all – but most.

Which would be the two most important of the above to you? Of course, I may be mistaken, but if given a free choice, I would expect that you would choose mainly if not only from the right-hand column. Notice too, that just thinking about your choices from that column, you actually feel better about yourself.

That is interesting isn't it - because most of us have been conditioned and in fact tend in practice to apply most of our energy towards the types of things listed in the left column! In 'the West', our societies are mostly geared up towards and prioritise those things found in the left column. Materialism is our religion. We are encouraged to dedicate our lives towards earning money and acquiring things with it. Thus, the Internet and Shopping Centre has become the modern church or synagogue.

Of course, I also suspect that whilst making choices from the right-hand column, you are aware of the little voice in your head that is saying 'yes but I would be happy if I had lots of money'.

But would you be? Are people who have fame and/or great financial wealth truly happy? Are they deeply and lastingly happy? Are they free from fear, anxiety, insecurity, depression and worries?

Were they deeply and lastingly happy in giving their energies towards the goals of success, fame and wealth?

I do not know, but I imagine that many of the people that we all see in the news and on television who are wealthy and/or famous are gifted and have worked extremely hard to achieve their 'success'.

But it is never enough. Even they will eventually acknowledge something within themselves that says – 'what I have is great, but there must be more to life than this'.

Think how many famous people from the worlds of music, sport, film and business at some point turn towards 'religion' or spiritual guidance.

They are not alone.

We may not all succeed in acquiring vast material wealth or fame but from a young age we are all encouraged to try. Even so, when we think about it carefully, we acknowledge that such pursuit does not provide deep and lasting happiness. At best, it provides a sense of achievement that is short lived and seems to spur us on for more in the deluded belief that we will eventually find happiness.

It is in vain hope that with more effort we will produce more money that will buy more 'things' that will produce more happiness. But as we come to experience this process we realize that it is like chasing a shadow. The pursuit of happiness through material means brings us no real fulfilment; therefore, the things that we are conditioned to believe are valuable and immediately tangible are but only short lived.

Where then do we look for that deep and lasting happiness that always seems to come within our grasp only to slip away like water through our hands?

You know there is an answer and you are searching for it. You believe in God. You believe that God can provide the answer.

The answer is like the Holy Grail - a secret and mysterious holy vessel. But where can it be found?

Something inside you tells you that the answer is close at hand and that if you look in the right place you will find it. I can absolutely assure you that you are right - it is within your reach.

You are determined to find it, and you feel that by continuing with your path that you will find what you are looking for. You can and you will.

If you are fortunate, you may have had glimpses of it already. For me it came as a sort of momentary intense flash of insight that gives a feeling of euphoria, of overwhelming peace and love. It is a state of no fear. It is a feeling of space, knowing, freedom, expansion, abundance and creativity. It is a state of true love toward all things and all people. It makes you cry – not out of joy or pain – but of love and relief.

But the glimpse quickly faded and became a faint memory. You then want to experience it more often. In fact, you want to have that 'feeling' all of the time. Now that you have had that experience, you want to know where it came from, what took it away and how, when can you find it again, in order that you can hold on to it.

In the Zen Buddhist tradition this momentary 'insight' is called 'Satori' – a word that is often translated as 'enlightenment'. It is a glimpse behind the curtain into the Light. It is a higher level of consciousness or awareness.

In Christianity, enlightenment is called 'the Kingdom of Heaven' or 'the Kingdom of God' - and in modern Kabbalah, it is called the 'Ninety Nine'. These are all words trying to explain the same thing.

In each case it is a glimpse of a state of being that is beyond adequate description – but deep down you know it is what you want, what you need and what you are looking for.

After all – when asked, your preferred choice was to direct your energies towards spiritual goals – not material ones. You know how you felt inside when you considered the choices and how 'good' you felt just by considering and choosing only from the spiritual column. Look at them again (page 29) carefully and recover that feeling.

The question is – 'How do I achieve those goals and still 'survive' in the real world? How do I find that balance and deep and lasting happiness? Can I find that balance and still enjoy deep and lasting happiness? You can if you try and apply yourself properly.

That is the hidden treasure buried within you. The challenge is firstly finding the treasure and then making it your life.

"The Kingdom of Heaven* is like treasure hidden in a field. When a man found it, he hid it again, and then in his joy went and sold all he had and bought that field."

[Matthew 13:44]

* Higher Consciousness/ Ninety Nine/ The Light/ Enlightenment/ Nirvana/ Kingdom of God

I believe that you are that field - the vessel in which the treasure of happiness is hidden and can be found. Happiness cannot be found outside of you.

I also believe that if you follow your path, you will find that treasure and when you do, like 'the man', you will live your life focused on the Treasure to the virtual exclusion of all other things that were formerly of value to you.

You will come to change the way you look at life and the world. You will adjust your sights towards what is of real value.

And when you do that – you will have found Heaven on Earth – the Light - Enlightenment – Nirvana - and all the peace, love, joy, prosperity and abundance you need – and more.

Jesus & Kabbalah - Paths & Destination

I have no desire or intention of encouraging you to give up your path or beliefs - whether it be Judaism, Buddhism, Islam, Nothingism, Christianity and/or Kabbalah and/or something else.

All paths at times run parallel and at other times cross, but more importantly their true destinations are one and the same.

Nevertheless, the starting point must also be the same namely, the desire to find the Treasure.

In this book, I hope to show you that there is evidence in the New Testament that the person known as Jesus, the Jesus born around 7-4 BC, who lived and walked this Earth and was crucified around 28-36AD, knew of, practiced and preached Kabbalah.

I believe that the central teaching of Jesus as disclosed in the Synoptic Gospels and Kabbalah is without material difference. At first glance this may seem something of a bold assertion, however, it must always be remembered that Jesus was a Jew. Jesus was born a Jew into a Jewish family. He was circumcised. He had a bar mitzvah and became a Rabbi. According to the New Testament - Jesus had Jewish parents, brothers, sisters, cousins, aunts and uncles. His disciples and early followers were all Jews. They were not 'Christians'.

Jesus is recognized by Jews and Christians as being well versed in the Torah, and he often quoted from it. He is known to have attended and taught, argued and even healed in synagogues. He conversed with other Rabbis, observed Jewish feasts and ultimately was assassinated at the behest of the Jewish Sanhedrin – the Court of Judges or religious leaders and interpreters of the Law – the Torah and the 'Old Testament'.

Let us look at this another way and in particular look at what the Synoptic Gospels did not report Jesus as teaching.

In the Synoptic Gospels and in the Gospel of Mark in particular <u>Jesus is not reported as teaching</u>:

- The Doctrine of the Holy Trinity.
- The Doctrine of Substantiation.
- You must recognise a priest as being necessary to intercede between you and God.
- (For almost two thousand years) – the Jews are responsible for my death.
- Priests must be celibate.
- You must have a Pope or an Archbishop.
- You must accept Rome or Canterbury or indeed anywhere as the 'headquarters' of my teachings.
- You must go to Church on Sunday.
- You must participate in a daily or weekly ritual known as 'the Mass' or 'Service'.
- You must attend Confession before a priest.
- You must recognise the New Testament books as the only books that are the authentic 'word of God' - to the exclusion of others.
- You must create the Sunday Missal, follow the Order of Service and the cycle of liturgy to be read at Mass.
- You must recite the Creed.
- You must accept as Mortal and/or Venal sins those which are chosen by the Roman Catholic

Church, how and when and by who sins should be forgiven – or indeed if they can be forgiven.

- You must say the Mass in Latin, in English or some other colloquial language.
- The New Testament shall only be in Latin.

The list could go on. I invite you to look in the Synoptic Gospels and see if you can discover where any of these things are taught by Jesus at all or in the way that they are taught by organised Christian and/or Jewish religions.

All of these things would be unknown to Jesus and his followers. Indeed, as I shall show in this book what Jesus taught tended towards the opposite of each of these things.

In the end, Jesus was crucified not least in part as a result of his declarations against the over emphasis of the same types of practices that he found in the Judaism of his time, as we can observe in 'Christian' churches and synagogues today! This is not to say that organised religion, priests and certain doctrine cannot help in the pursuit of spiritual goals. They can and often do. But at all times, it is important to be conscious of differentiating between a religion and the people who populate it and the hidden spiritual treasure. The former is at most the signpost towards the latter. Organised religion maybe the means to the end but certainly not the end itself.

It can be uncomfortable to realize that the very things that Jesus observed in the organised religion of his time (Judaism), which he repeatedly criticises - was subsequently perpetuated by the Christian communities and churches - ostensibly in his name.

However, it is also exciting to understand this since it enables us to claim back the real Jesus and his original, inspiring teaching. Under the many layers of ritual and the demand to comply with organized religion, there is something much more simple, profound and liberating.

We can share the joy and enthusiasm that his contemporary listeners experienced when they remarked:

'Where did this man get all this?''

[Mark 6:2]

That is a good question.

The connection between Judaism and Jesus, the Jewish Rabbi who taught in the synagogues and the Temple in Jerusalem throughout his ministry – cannot be over emphasized.

As I will explain, it is a fundamental declaration in the Synoptic Gospels that Jesus was affirming the very essence of Judaism.

Kabbalah

For hundreds of years prior to the birth of Jesus, Judaism was essentially focussed around the Torah. This 'book' contains the first five books of what Christians call the Old Testament. – that is to say, Genesis, Exodus, Leviticus, Numbers and Deuteronomy. The Torah also came to mean more than the first five books and is a word that describes all of the scriptures in what is known as 'the Hebrew Bible'. This is what Christians call the 'Old Testament'.

For mainstream orthodox Jews from before the time of Jesus right up to the present day – the true and deeper meaning of the Torah is contained within what is nowadays called Kabbalah.

Kabbalah literally means in Hebrew 'receiving tradition'. It is a body of knowledge that has been handed down the ages from and to specially chosen Rabbis – one to the next generation.

Kabbalah seeks to explain the hidden and true meaning of the Torah – the Hebrew Bible. Kabbalah teaches that the Torah when properly understood and in modern parlance 'de-coded' - explains the concept of God the Creator of all things and that which has been created. According to Kabbalah the events depicted in the Torah are not primarily records of actual events in history (though they may be), but are 'stories' that contain references to the nature of the universe and human beings; encompassing how and why we came into being and defining the relationship between us and that Creator.

Kabbalah sees that relationship as revolving around a connection to an energy called the 'Light' - that emanates from God. It is important to note that Kabbalah is not a religion of itself. Traditional practitioners of Kabbalah believe that Kabbalah's origins pre-date world religions. They say that it has existed in oral form since at least the beginning of the revelation of the Torah to Moses and long before. Indeed, Kabbalists believe that Kabbalah formed part of the revelation given to Moses on Mount Sinai. Some believe that it formed part of the body of knowledge passed onto Adam – the first man. When Kabbalah is properly understood, this is not as preposterous as it might at first seem.

According to Kabbalah, the oral tradition of Kabbalah was first committed to writing in two books, the first of which is called the Sefer Yitzirah (The Book of Formation) and the second of which is called 'the Zohar' (the Book of Splendour).

I discuss both books in chapter 4.

What is important from this book's perspective is this:

- Kabbalah is an esoteric (hidden) body of knowledge concerning the Torah and its long history is and always has been recognized by Orthodox Judaism as an integral part of Judaism.

- Kabbalah was definitely a part of Judaism at the time of Jesus. It was not then known as 'Kabbalah' but by other names.
- Kabbalah has a remarkable connection with Northern Galilee. The Rabbi who is said to have authored the Zohar in the 2nd Century is buried in Meron – only 20 miles from Capernaum and the Sea of Galilee – where much of Jesus's ministry is described in the Synoptic Gospels.
- Kabbalah was kept secret and hidden to all but a few devout and carefully chosen Rabbis. It was not discussed or taught to every Rabbi, 'ordinary Jews' and certainly not to Gentiles.
- At the time of Jesus, the disclosure of Kabbalah to the ordinary practicing Orthodox Jew and/or Gentiles would have incurred the wrath of the 'leaders' of organized 'orthodox' Judaism; and would have resulted in death to the discloser – and also his followers.

As I hope to show in this book, the teachings, metaphors and concepts of Kabbalah bear a striking resemblance to those we are told in the Synoptic Gospels were used by Jesus.

There may be several explanations for what was perceived by his listeners as a unique and striking 'authority' of Jesus. But Kabbalah is one of them and probably the most plausible.

If I am correct in saying that the central teaching of Jesus contains concepts that can be found in Kabbalah, the consequences could be far-reaching and profound.

From a historical point of view, almost all of what we know of what Jesus said and did is found in the New Testament of the Bible – in particular the Synoptic Gospels – Matthew, Mark and Luke.

Kabbalah has its roots and connections with the Torah and its foundational texts – the Sefer Yitzirah and the Zohar.

To find a connection between the teachings of Jesus and Kabbalah, we should therefore turn our attention to each of these books - the Synoptic Gospels, the Torah, the Sefir Yitzirah and the Zohar.

If we wish to rely upon what is said about Jesus, what he taught and did, it would be helpful to first understand the degree to which we can rely upon the primary historical source materials – the Synoptic Gospels. Having established that there may be a number of things within the Synoptic Gospels that we can rely upon, we can examine those things carefully. As we shall see, when we do so - what is revealed is a very simple, straightforward and profound teaching about happiness and where and how it can be found.

Before we can examine the treasure we must locate where it is buried. It will be important to establish a good foundation in and around the area of excavation before bringing the treasure into the light.

Chapter 3 –
The Torah & The Bible

The word 'Bible' is derived from Latin (Biblia) meaning 'the books' or a collection of books. That is what the Bible is – a collection of books by various and numerous authors.

To Christians, 'the Bible' comprises of both the 'Old Testament' and the 'New Testament' and I use the term 'Bible' with that understanding. The New Testament of course contains the four gospels of Matthew, Mark, Luke and John together with the Acts of the Apostles, the letters of St Paul and many other letters. What Christians and others know as the 'Old Testament' is in Judaism the Hebrew Bible - which comprises of the Torah and other scriptures.

The contents of the Old Testament and the Hebrew Bible are essentially the same but are not always in the same order; they are grouped and categorised differently and have different punctuation. Although I am going to explain a little more about each, for the purposes of this book and for convenience, I shall refer to the Torah, the Old Testament and the Hebrew Bible all as the Torah.

It is often assumed that the various books in the Bible were written in the order in which they appear in the Bible. But that is not the case. They are actually organised by subjects/topics and/or size. It is also erroneously presumed that the New Testament was in existence in its current form for the early Christians – those followers of Jesus who were present at his crucifixion and shortly after. It was not. Whilst the Synoptic Gospels (at least in oral form) were almost certainly widely known amongst the very early Christian communities, the New Testament as we know it today came into being hundreds of years later.

When and by whom the various books of the New Testament were written (i.e. the authors) has been the subject of considerable scholarly investigation and learning. This is a fascinating topic - but one which I will leave for another time. The bottom line is that nobody knows who the actual authors were and anyway, it is almost universally accepted by mainstream biblical academics that no one person wrote all that is contained within each book.

Moreover, the circumstances in which these particular books came to be comprised in the New Testament as opposed to several other similar contemporaneous books dealing with the same or similar narratives, is an interesting topic in and of itself. But it is a contentious subject and whilst some aspects of it have some bearing on what I am discussing here, I will make only a brief incursion into its murky depths.

The books of the New Testament were finally designated by the Catholic Church as forming the definitive holy scripture (cannon), by men (not women) from a number of possible books some 200 – 300 years after the books were originally written (and Jesus had died) - and after many and prolonged arguments – often violent between different factions of 'the Church'.

Some of the differences and emphasis in each of the books in the New Testament can be accounted for by the fact that the author(s) was addressing different audiences.

For example, the author might be trying to persuade a Jew of the 'Jewishness' of Jesus and so emphasise that aspect. In contrast, another might be directing his or her writing to the Gentiles (Non-Jews) and to make the teaching relevant to them.

Writing around 226 AD, one of the "fathers of the church" Origen of Alexandria and Caesarea wrote in his "commentary on Matthew";

"As I have understood from tradition, respecting the four gospels, which are the only and undisputed ones in the whole church of god under heaven. The first is written according to Matthew...who having published it for the Jewish converts, wrote it in the Hebrew. The second is according to Mark, who composed it, as Peter explained it to him, whom he also acknowledges as his son in his general Epistles...and the third according to Luke, the gospel commended by Paul, which was for the converts from the Gentiles, and last of all the gospel according to John." - [C.E. Hill, Who Chose the Gospels, p.46]

In each instance for fear of the consequences, the authors were careful to ensure that if what they wrote fell into the hands of the Romans – it did not offend their sensibilities.

In the case of the Christian Church, the arguments and violence concerning which books and which versions of the books should form part of the cannon of the New Testament caused divisions (schisms) and ultimately is reflected in the different versions of the Bible; these variations in the beliefs and practices are seen in the various denominations of 'Christian' churches today.

It follows therefore that in deciding what the true followers were permitted to read, some books were left out of different versions of different Bibles. At least one book – the Gospel of St. Thomas – is generally thought by theologians and academics alike to be worthy of inclusion in all versions of the New Testament. But it is not. The reasons for its continued exclusion are opaque.

There are also several other candidates for inclusion, however, the Gospel of Thomas is particularly interesting and useful as a means for reaching the recorded sayings of Jesus. The Gospel does not appear to have been subjected to the same degree (if any) of redaction and editing as the Synoptic Gospels. Thus, it acts as a useful yardstick for authenticity as to what Jesus taught. But since it does not form part of the Christian canon I do not use it here to show the links with Kabbalah.

The Old Testament in the Bible used by Catholics and Eastern Orthodox churches is different from most Protestant versions. The Protestant Bible has seven less books than the Catholic Bible. Protestants decided to exclude the seven books at the time of the Reformation in and around 1517.

In addition to the twenty-four Books of the Protestant Old Testament, the Roman Catholic Bible includes, (1) Tobit, (2) Judith, (3) Wisdom of Solomon, (4) Ecclesiasticus (Sirach), (5) Baruch (includes Letters of Jeremiah), (6 & 7) Maccabees 1 & 2. These seven books are called the deuterocanonical books. There are also slight differences by way of additions to the books of Esther and Daniel.

The decision to retain these seven books (and other religious dogma) was made at a meeting of the leaders of the Roman Catholic Church in Trento (Trent) and Bologna in Northern Italy, between 1545 and 1563. This meeting is known as the Council of Trent. Yes, one thousand five hundred years after the death of Jesus, the Catholic Church was still considering what should and should not form part of the Bible. However, the 'New Testaments' of each of the Protestant, Catholic and Eastern Orthodox religions contain the same twenty-seven books. In principle, there is no reason why today the current version of the Catholic Bible and indeed all Christian Bibles could not be amended by deletion or addition. There are good reasons to suggest that it should be amended – but again that is for another day.

It may come as a surprise to learn that what we now know to be the 'New Testament' has not always been entirely in its present form. Indeed, the two oldest known manuscript versions of the Greek Bible (Old and New Testament) written in the fourth century are held in the Vatican vaults and the British Museum. They are known respectively as 'Codex Vaticanus' and 'Codex Sinaiticus'. Neither of these two versions contain the story of the woman caught in adultery recorded in the Gospel of John 8:1-11. It would seem that this story was added much later – again hundreds of years later.

Moreover, even now words used in one Christian Bible are not exactly the same in each of them – both as a result of different translations but also words left in and words left out when they were copied.

For the purposes of this book, I have used the New Revised Standard Version of the Bible. This is generally recognised by both religious authorities and academics as a if not the most reliable translation of the Bible into English. In any event, any differences between the New Revised Standard Version of the Bible and other versions do not affect the issues that I am discussing. In the case of the first five books of the Torah, I have also used the translation and commentary of the late Rabbi Aryeh Kaplan in his book 'The Living Torah'.

'Old' & 'New' - Testaments

The Bible of Christians of course comprises of the 'Old Testament' and the 'New Testament'. The epithet 'Old Testament' is not something that Judaism immediately recognizes and what might be called 'main stream' or orthodox Judaism did not and does not recognize the 'New Testament', or rather the message contained within it, as part of Judaism's body of beliefs.

Kabbalah however, does recognise and accept Jesus as a prophet and also his core teachings. But to be clear, Kabbalists are not 'Christians'. But then again, Jesus wasn't a Christian. That doesn't mean to say however, that a Christian cannot be a Kabbalist either. There are many Christians who are also Kabbalists. I was once introduced to a Spanish Catholic at the London Kabbalah Centre who claimed to be a descendent of a Renaissance Pope.

For Judaism, the 'Old Testament' is a collection of the writings (holy scriptures) known as the TaNaCH – 'Tanach'.

TaNaCH includes:

'Ta' - 'the Torah' (Genesis, Exodus, Leviticus, Numbers and Deuteronomy)

'Na' - is for 'Neviim' (Prophets – e.g. Isaiah, Daniel, Elijah)

'CH' - is for 'Kituvim' (Writings) that includes Psalms, poetry and many more.

To make matters a little more confusing, even within Judaism, 'the Torah' which is really the First five books as mentioned, is sometimes referred to as the Torah and the Prophets and the writings – in other words, everything that Christians call the Old Testament!

As I said earlier, I am going to adopt the same approach and so when I say 'the Torah' it will mean the Tanack (TaNaCH) - what Christians call the Old Testament – or the Hebrew Bible.

The Gospels

The New Testament is so called because Christians say it is the new 'covenant' or new 'agreement' instituted between God and Jesus, not just on behalf of Israel but on behalf of both Jews <u>and</u> Gentiles (non-Jews).

The 'old' covenant (or agreement) was first instituted between God and Abraham [Genesis 12:1-3]. There were of course subsequent covenants with Noah, Moses and David.

But as I shall show later, the so-called 'new covenant' is not really a new covenant as it is based on a fundamental misunderstanding of:

I. What in common parlance has been the designation of the Jews as the 'chosen race' or chosen/specially/solely appointed people of God – to the exclusion of all others; and

II. The core message of Jesus as recorded in the New Testament

The primary books of the New Testament are the four 'Gospels' of Matthew, Mark, Luke and John, together with the Acts of the Apostles ['Acts'] and the many letters written by St. Paul and his followers.

The word 'Gospel' is derived from Old English 'god-spell' meaning 'good news'.

As I shall later show, according to Jesus himself (as recorded in the Synoptic Gospels) - the good news is delivered by Jesus but solely concerns Metanoia and the Kingdom of God.

It is also clear from the Synoptic Gospels that the good news is not Jesus - but his teaching, his message.

Almost 600 years before the birth of Jesus, the prophet Jeremiah reported in the Torah the words of an oracle of the Lord:

"The days are coming when I will make a <u>new covenant</u> with the house of Israel and the house of Judah. It will not be like the covenant with their ancestors the day when I took them by the hand to lead them forth from the land of Egypt....I will place

my law <u>within them</u> and write it upon their hearts. I will be their God and they shall be my people"

[Jer 31:31 – 33]

[My emphasis]

As the respected Roman Catholic Christian biblical scholar Raymond E. Brown said, "New" here has a connotation of "renewed" even though the renewal is "not like the covenant made with their ancestor"; it may have had that force when first used by the believers in Jesus.

In the New Testament in Matthew 5:17, Jesus is reported as saying:

'Do not think that I have come to abolish the law or the prophets; I have come not to abolish but to fulfil'.

Where is that law to be found? The law that Jesus refers to is found in the Torah – the Hebrew Bible.

In **Mark** 12:28 we are told that when asked by a scribe;

"Which commandment is the first of all?"

Jesus replied:

"The first of all commandments is, Hear, O Israel; The Lord our God is one; you shall love the Lord

your God with all your heart, and with all your soul, and with all your mind, and with all your strength."

"The second is this, 'You shall love your neighbour as yourself. There is no other commandment greater than these"

Jesus is quoting from Deuteronomy 6: 4-7 and Leviticus 19:18 – respectively the fifth and third books in the Torah.

The Gospel according to Mark

The Gospel according to Mark by scholarly consent was written around 60 - 75 AD, approximately 30 years after the death of Jesus.

The Catholic Church and all mainstream academics of all Christian denominations accept that Mark was the first of the four canonical books of the New Testament (Matthew, Mark, Luke and John) to be written. Matthew appears first in the New Testament because it is the longest.

Indeed, Mark by scholarly consent is the 'book' that is the main (but not only) source of what is written in Mathew and Luke - both of which were written 10 – 30 years after Mark. The three books (Mark, Matthew & Luke) are known as the Synoptic Gospels. If they are each laid side-by-side they would the same (syn) – look (optic) – hence 'synoptic'. – i.e. look the same.

Biblical scholars have discovered that it is likely that there is at least one other source of material common to the Gospels of Matthew and Luke – material that is not found in Mark. The identity of that source is unknown but in academic biblical circles that source is known as 'Q' – from the German word 'Quelle' meaning 'source'.

In the view of biblical scholars, that source possibly accounts for a significant portion of the two gospels – about 220 – 235 verses.

The consensus among mainstream academics is that:

- The Synoptic Gospels contain more 'historical' information as to what Jesus said and did compared to the Gospel of John [and indeed the rest of the New Testament]; and
- Mark contains the most reliable history of the three.

The Gospel according to John was written somewhere between 90-110 AD. It is for the main part a discrete work; and whilst to some extent purports to be based on what Jesus said and did, the book is more of an exposition of who and what Jesus represented to the author, rather than a piece of work that's purpose is to accurately record historical events. The Gospel according to John is a different interpretation of the teaching of Jesus than what is immediately apparent in the Synoptic Gospels.

Ironically, the contents of the Gospel of John very closely resemble the teachings of Kabbalah but because of its historical unreliability, I am not using this as supporting evidence of the connection between Jesus and Kabbalah. (I will deal with this in a separate book in due course).

However, for curiosity's sake, a very brief examination and comparison of John and Kabbalah might be interesting for setting the scene for what's later to come when comparing the Synoptic Gospels and Kabbalah. Let me give you an example of the Kabbalah references in the Gospel of John. Below is John 3:1-21 and the emphasis is mine.

Now there was a Pharisee named Nicodemus, a leader of the Jews. He came to Jesus <u>by night</u> and said to him, 'Rabbi, we know that you are <u>a teacher who has come from God</u>; for no one can do <u>these signs</u> that you do apart from the presence of God.' Jesus answered him, 'Very truly, I tell you, <u>no one can see the Kingdom of God without being born from above.</u>' Nicodemus said to him, '<u>How can anyone be born after having grown old? Can one enter a second time into the mother's womb and be born?</u>' Jesus answered, 'Very truly, I tell you, <u>no one can enter the Kingdom of God without being born of water and Spirit. What is born of the flesh is flesh, and what is born of the Spirit is spirit.</u> Do not be astonished that I said to you, <u>"You must be born from above."</u> The <u>wind blows</u> where it chooses, and you <u>hear the sound</u> of it, but you do not know where it comes from or

where it goes. So it is with everyone who is <u>born of the Spirit</u>.' Nicodemus said to him, 'How can these things be?' Jesus answered him, 'Are you a teacher of Israel, and yet you do not understand these things? 'Very truly, I tell you, we speak of what we know and testify to what we have seen; yet you do not receive our testimony. If I have told you about <u>earthly things</u> and you do not believe, how can you believe if I tell you about <u>heavenly things</u>? No one has <u>ascended into heaven</u> except the one who descended from heaven, the <u>Son of Man</u>. And just as Moses lifted up the serpent in the wilderness, so must the <u>Son of Man be lifted up</u>...'

It is the first of the important Johannine dialogues. This Pharisee, a member of the Sanhedrin, comes to Jesus **'at night'** because he does not yet belong to the light, and the Pharisee acknowledges him as **'a teacher who has come from God''**. What Nicodemus represents is an inadequate faith, as becomes evident when Jesus explains that only begetting from above enables one to enter the Kingdom of God, i.e. begetting of water and Spirit. The Jesus that John portrays is the life of God acquired only when one is begotten by God **'from above'**, which takes place when one is baptized in water and receives God's Spirit. Jesus is talking about spiritual birth and spiritual life.

Nicodemus is alluding to natural birth from a Jewish mother that makes one a member of the chosen people, a people that the Torah considers God's child (See: Exodus 4:22; Deuteronomy 32:6; Hosea 11:10).

John rejects this at 3:6 for the only thing that flesh can beget or give birth to, is flesh. (Beget means to father or produce off spring.)

The Jesus John depicts is radically replacing what constitutes the children of God, challenging any privileged status stemming from natural Jewish parenthood.

This latter point is fundamental to Kabballah.

Indeed, to a Kabbalist there are many references to Kabbalah in this passage alone and I will be looking at some of them later in this book as they arise in the context of the Synoptic Gospels.

But I do not rely on the Gospel of John for the purpose of this book. It is not as historically reliable as the Gospel of Mark. We cannot be at all certain that this dialogue between Jesus and Nicodemus actually occurred. The passages that immediately follow appear to be in the nature of an exposition of later Christian theology and therefore somewhat self-serving.

Jesus did not write any of the books that are found in the New Testament. Nor did he edit any. He did not select which books were included or excluded from the New Testament. He did not review and approve what was written about him. He did not rely upon the New Testament and in particular the Synoptic Gospels as the basis of his message or his teaching.

Jesus was first and foremost a Rabbi who spoke to and with people from all aspects of his Jewish society. If Jesus relied upon any written material, it was that which is found in the Torah. Indeed, he is reported in the New Testament and the Synoptic Gospels in particular - as quoting from the Torah on a number of occasions.

However, there appears to have been something very different and outstanding both about what he said and how he said it, since this too is reported on many occasions in each of the Synoptic Gospels. On several occasions the Synoptic Gospels report how Jesus speaks with an 'authority' that is both perplexing and yet astounding. It seems these reports point to something that he knows that others do not.

This is noted in the very first Chapter of the Gospel of Mark – the first and earliest of the Synoptic Gospels:

'He entered the synagogue and taught. They were astounded at his teaching, for he taught as one having authority, and not as the scribes'.

[Mark 1:21]

But there are many examples in the Gospels of these qualities being remarked upon and here is a small selection to support this point.

"They were all amazed and they kept asking one another ''What is this? A new teaching – with authority!''.' [Mark 1:27]

"On the Sabbath he began to teach in the synagogue, and many who heard him were astounded. They said, ''Where did this man get all this? What is the <u>wisdom</u> that has been given to him?''

[Mark 6:2]

The observation is repeated in both Matthew and Luke.

"Now when Jesus had finished saying these things the crowd were astounded at his teaching for he taught as one having authority, and not as their scribes."

[Matthew 6:28]

'He went down to Capernaum, a city in Galilee, and was teaching them on the Sabbath. They were astounded at this teaching because he spoke with <u>authority</u>'.

[Luke 4:32]

It would seem clear that what Jesus is reported as teaching is something that is not simply contained in the Torah for that would have been what the scribes taught. What is noticed is not just that Jesus taught with authority but that he taught something that had not been taught before. Equally, the content, wisdom and the teaching had a substantial impact on his audience. They were 'astounded'.

If we are to believe what is being said in each of the Synoptic Gospels, Jesus knew something that was hidden, secret and unique. But more importantly he was apparently sharing that 'something' with those who listened to him. But it was not just what Jesus said that astonished and surprised his contemporaries. It is what he is said to have done. I am of course referring to the miracles that feature a great deal throughout the Synoptic Gospels. I discuss those in more detail in Chapter 8.

Jesus seems to have had unique gifts and insights from an early age. The first reported reference to these gifts is recorded in Luke. It is not mentioned in Mark or Matthew and so we should view what is said with some caution. Even so, it is not inconsistent with the points made above and in later chapters of this book.

"Every year his parents went to Jerusalem for the Festival of the Passover. And when he was <u>twelve years old</u>, they went up as usual to the festival. When the festival ended and they started to return the boy Jesus stayed behind in Jerusalem, but his parents did not know it. Assuming he was in the group of travellers, they went a day's journey. Then they started to look for him among their relatives and friends. When they did not find him they returned to Jerusalem to search for him. After three days they found him in the temple, sitting among the teachers, listening to them and asking them questions. And all who heard him were amazed at his understanding and his answers. When his parents saw him they were astonished and his mother said to him ''Child, why

have you treated us like this? Your father and I have been searching for you in great anxiety''. He said to them ''Why were you searching for me? Did you not know that I must be in my father's house?'' But they did not understand what he said to them. Then he went down with them and came to Nazareth and was obedient to them. His mother treasured all these things in her heart.
And Jesus increased in wisdom and in years and in divine and human favour.'

[Luke 2:41-52]

It is likely but not known with absolute certainty that 1st century Jewish practice meant that religious instruction would have become more intense for a boy from the age of twelve.

Indeed there is evidence from within Kabbalah that gifted young boys were singled out for special teaching. Rabbi Ishmael "Ba'al HaBaraita" or Ishmael ben Elisha (90-135 AD) is a recognized Jewish sage; he is believed to be buried in Parod in Northern Galilee. He was also a Kabbalist.

In his book 'Meditation and Kabbalah', Rabbi Aryeh Kaplan notes from what is recorded in the Midrash*:

'Rabbi Ishmael said: ''I was thirteen years old when I went to study with Rabbi Nehuniah ben Hakanah''

*The Midrash is the genre of rabbinic literature which contains early interpretations and commentaries on the Written Torah and Oral Torah. I will explain more about this later.

Rabbi Nehuniah ben Hakanah was a Kabbalist.

According to the passage in the Gospel of Luke, at the age of twelve Jesus is already showing signs of insight and wisdom that is beyond his years. He is a prodigy. In the Synoptic Gospels, there is a gap between this event when Jesus is twelve years and the beginning of his ministry when he was probably around thirty years old. No one knows where Jesus lived or what he did during this period.

There has been a great deal of speculation about these 'missing years'. The answer may simply be that he was studying the Torah and Kabbalah under the guidance of a recognized sage. This seems a possible and certainly a rational explanation for a great deal of what is described in the Synoptic Gospels.

Let me provide you with what the Kabbalist Rabbi Ishmael went on to say as recorded in the Midrash. It is evident that there are a number of parallels with what is recorded in the Synoptic Gospels concerning Jesus:
"I was already fasting, but I decided to increase my mortification. I separated myself from all enjoyment for an additional forty days, beyond my previous fasts. At the end of the forty days, I pronounced the Great Name and brought down the angel Yofiel. He descended into a flaming fire, and his face was like a

flash of lightening…He said to me, "Son of man, how dare you agitate the great Assembly on high?"

I fortified myself and replied, "It is known and revealed before the One who spoke and brought the world into being that I did not bring you down to earth for my own honour, but only to do the will of your Master"…After I had done this, he taught me a Divine Name, with which I would ascend and descend."

Compare the above passage concerning Rabbi Ishmael and what is written in the Gospels of Mark, Matthew and Luke with respect to Jesus – Rabbi Yeshua (Joshua):

> "And the Spirit immediately drove him out into the wilderness. 13 He was in the wilderness forty days, tempted by Satan; and he was with the wild beasts; and the angels waited on him."

[Mark 1]

Then Jesus was led up by the Spirit into the wilderness to be tempted by the devil. He fasted forty days and forty nights, and afterwards he was famished. The tempter came and said to him, "If you are the Son of God, command these stones to become loaves of bread." But he answered, "It is written,
'One does not live by bread alone,
but by every word that comes from the mouth of God.'"

Then the devil took him to the holy city and placed him on the pinnacle of the temple, saying to him, "If you are the Son of God, throw yourself down; for it is written,

'He will command his angels concerning you,'

and 'On their hands they will bear you up,

so that you will not dash your foot against a stone.'"

Jesus said to him, "Again it is written, 'Do not put the Lord your God to the test.'"

Again, the devil took him to a very high mountain and showed him all the Kingdoms of the world and their splendour; and he said to him, "All these I will give you, if you will fall down and worship me." Jesus said to him, "Away with you, Satan! for it is written,

'Worship the Lord your God,

and serve only him.'

Then the devil left him, and suddenly angels came and waited on him."

[Matthew 4]

"Jesus, full of the Holy Spirit, returned from the Jordan and was led by the Spirit in the wilderness, where for forty days he was tempted by the devil. He ate nothing at all during those days, and when they were over, he was famished. The devil said to him, "If you are the Son of God, command this stone to become a loaf of bread." Jesus answered him, "It is written, 'One does not live by bread alone.'"

Then the devil led him up and showed him in an instant all the Kingdoms of the world. And the devil said to him, "To you I will give their glory and all this

authority; for it has been given over to me, and I give it to anyone I please. If you, then, will worship me, it will all be yours." Jesus answered him, "It is written,
'Worship the Lord your God,
and serve only him.'"
Then the devil took him to Jerusalem, and placed him on the pinnacle of the temple, saying to him, "If you are the Son of God, throw yourself down from here, for it is written,
'He will command his angels concerning you,
to protect you,'
and
'On their hands they will bear you up,
so that you will not dash your foot against a stone.'"
Jesus answered him, It is said, 'Do not put the Lord your God to the test.' When the devil had finished every test, he departed from him until an opportune time."

[Luke 4]

In the former passage from Luke, there is an important detail that is written and which perhaps gives a clue as to a connection with Kabbalah. This is something that to Jesus' later listeners, may have appeared somewhat surprising and unintelligible.

Jesus refers to God as 'Abba' אבא meaning 'Father' in Aramaic.

Abba has particular significance in Kabbalah – as I shall later reveal and detail.

However, now that we have spent some time considering the Bible, the Torah, the New Testament and the Synoptic Gospels, before looking in detail at what Jesus taught with 'authority', let us first turn to Kabbalah and to its two foundational texts – the Sefer Yitzirah and the Zohar – respectively the Book of Formation and the Book of Splendour.

Chapter 4 –
An Introduction to Kabbalah

To introduce and better understand Kabbalah and its connection with the Synoptic Gospels, a good place to start is at the beginning of the Zohar, one of Kabbalah's main foundational texts.

The very first lines of the Zohar are as follows:

Original Aramaic

1. רִבִּי חִזְקַיָּה פָּתַח, כְּתִיב כְּשׁוֹשַׁנָּה בֵּין הַחוֹחִים. מָאן שׁוֹשַׁנָּה, דָּא כְּנֶסֶת יִשְׂרָאֵל. בְּגִין דְּאִית שׁוֹשַׁנָּה וְאִית שׁוֹשַׁנָּה, מַה שׁוֹשַׁנָּה דְּאִיהִי בֵּין הַחוֹחִים אִית בַּהּ סוּמָק וְחִוָּור, אוּף כְּנֶסֶת יִשְׂרָאֵל אִית בַּהּ דִּין וְרַחֲמֵי. מַה שׁוֹשַׁנָּה אִית בַּהּ תְּלֵיסַר עָלִין, אוּף כְּנֶסֶת יִשְׂרָאֵל אִית בַּהּ תְּלֵיסַר מְכִילִין דְּרַחֲמֵי דְּסַחֲרִין לַהּ מִכָּל סִטְרָהָא. אוּף אֱלֹהִים דְּהָכָא מִשַּׁעְתָּא דְּאִדְכַּר אַפִּיק תְּלֵיסַר תֵּיבִין לְסַחֲרָא לִכְנֶסֶת יִשְׂרָאֵל וּלְנַטְרָא לַהּ.

Translation

1. Rabbi Chizkiyah opened the discussion with the verse, "As the Lily among the thorns" (Shir Hashirim 2:2). HE ASKS: What is the Lily? AND HE REPLIES: It is the Congregation of Yisrael, WHICH IS MALCHUT. Because there is a Lily; and there is a Lily. Just as the Lily among

69

the thorns is tinged with red and white, so is the Congregation of Yisrael affected by the qualities of Judgment and Mercy. Just as the Lily has thirteen petals, so the Congregation of Yisrael is surrounded by the thirteen attributes of Mercy. Thus, between the first mention of the name Elohim, WHICH APPEARS IN THE PASSAGE, "IN THE BEGINNING ELOHIM CREATED" (BERESHEET 1:1) TO THE SECOND MENTION OF ELOHIM, THERE ARE THIRTEEN WORDS IN THE VERSE, WHICH TRANSLATE AS "THE, HEAVEN, AND THE, EARTH, AND THE EARTH, WAS, WITHOUT FORM, AND VOID, AND DARKNESS, WAS UPON, THE FACE, OF THE DEEP, AND A WIND" (IBID. 2). These words surround and guard the Congregation of Yisrael.

[N.B. The words in capitals are additional interpretations/explanations by the Kabbalah Centre].

(Prologue, Book 1, The Zohar)

In introducing this verse from the Zohar, the explanation given by Rabbi Philip Berg (the founder of the Kabbalah Centre) is this:

"The secret of spiritual protection is revealed through a richly metaphorical discourse given by Rabbi Chizkiyah. The Rabbi explains that the spiritual forces that protect and watch over us are called the Thirteen Attributes of Mercy. They are transmitted into our physical world through the first thirteen words of the Torah. When judgments are

decreed against us, these forces can safeguard us from their influence. We begin drawing this Light of protection to ourselves at the very moment we begin to browse and behold the mystical shapes and sequences of the Aramaic text, and to learn the spiritual insights presented there."

In light of the above, now read the following passage from the Gospel of Matthew. It is best known to Christians as the Sermon on the Mount. Remember, Jesus could have chosen any of the flowers growing in that region at that time:

"Consider the lilies of the field, how they grow; they neither toil nor spin, yet I tell you, even Solomon in all his glory was not clothed like one of these. But if God so clothes the grass of the field, which is alive today and tomorrow is thrown into the oven, will he not much more clothe you—you of little faith? Therefore do not worry, saying, 'What will we eat?' or 'What will we drink?' or 'What will we wear?' For it is the Gentiles who strive for all these things; and indeed your heavenly Father knows that you need all these things. But strive first for the Kingdom of God and his righteousness, and all these things will be given to you as well."

[Matthew 6.28-33]

Kabbalah is not a religion. It does not claim to be the one and only way to communicate with God and to achieve spiritual enlightenment. It is a guide that makes itself available to everyone that wishes to utilize its knowledge and wisdom.

You will not be banned or excommunicated if you do not agree with and/or adhere to what Kabbalah teaches. Kabbalah is a body of knowledge and a way of life. In modern parlance it is an instruction manual, a user guide, an operating system to understand God's world as set out in the Torah.

The word 'kabbalah' in Hebrew קבלה literally means 'receiving/tradition.' It is the receiving and passing on of a 'tradition' or a large body of secret knowledge with the principal aim of fulfilling two primary commandments from God, the ultimate source of all things – namely:

1. Loving God; and
2. Loving your neighbour

In actuality, the first commandment states to be in fear of God, however, fear in the sense of awe not fear in its usual sense, i.e. being frightened.

To properly and fully be in awe of God, one should be:

- Humbled by; and
- Appreciative of; and
- In love with

- not only the power that has brought everything into being but also all that has been brought into being.

The Torah and Kabbalah and the teaching of Jesus all point to these two fundamental 'commandments'. They are guiding principles to the means of a life lived in happiness and without fear. Another way of putting this is to say that the two commandments point to heaven here on earth. The essence of the teaching of the Torah, Kabbalah and Jesus is one and the same.

As recorded in the Synoptic Gospels, everything that Jesus said and did ultimately all point back to the Two Commandments. The same points are simply illustrated in different contexts. This too, is what should be understood when reading the Torah and Kabbalah texts. Everything is a tool, that helps point and give guidance to what in Kabbalah is called - the 'Tree of Life' or the 'Light'. To a Kabbalist, the Torah can only be properly understood and applied to everyday life,—with the assistance of Kabbalah. When read in conjunction with Kabbalah, the Torah provides the means to understanding the nature of existence and the relationship between Elohim (God – the Creator, the Source of All) and all created things – including and especially human beings.

It is important to bear in mind that like the Torah and the Synoptic Gospels, Kabbalah was not originally a written body of work. It was held in the memory of particular individuals who were trained to learn and recite vast numbers of words - and repeat them orally to enable each generation to pass onto the next. For modern human beings this seems almost impossible. But perhaps this is because over time most of us have lost the ability to memorise large bodies of text and numbers. Once it became possible to mass-produce paper, print books or store in a computer, the need to commit knowledge to memory became ever more redundant.

Our education system in the West places little value on human memory of factual information - but rather emphasizes the ability to remember where to find information (mostly books and the internet) and to some extent how to interpret and apply it.

When we read the Ancient Greek texts such as Homer's epic poems and the various other Greek myths and legends, we are reading what was originally stories memorised and repeated by story-tellers, the Bards. This technique of remembrance and recall is still exhibited in many societies throughout the world today, including the Aborigines, Native Americans, Hindus, Islamists and Buddhists.

In particular, this tradition has survived in Religious contexts. First there were the oral traditions and then later the written texts. The ability to commit large amounts of information to memory is extant even today. Actors can be called upon to memorise more than one play at a time. The famous physicist Professor Stephen Hawkins was forced through illness to memorise a vast amount of numbers and equations and was able to reflect upon them in his head – before committing them to written form.

In Islam, merit is obtained by anyone who learns by heart any of the verses of the Koran but especially those who learn all seventy-seven thousand words of the Koran. Such people are known as 'Hafiz', named after the Persian poet Khajeh Shamseddin Mohammad Hafiz-s Shiraz – who is said to have learned the Koran by heart in fourteen different ways. Even today the practice of learning the entire Koran is very much a part of Islamic culture.

In time - Kabbalah was also converted to writing.

At the heart of Kabbalah lies three main texts.

- The Torah
- The Book of Formation (Sefer Yetzirah) – this is also known as 'the Book of Abraham'
- The Book of Splendour (the Zohar)

Although inter-related, Kabbalah comprises of three elements:

- The theoretical or philosophical
- The meditative
- The magical

According to the world renowned Torah and Kabbalah scholar, Rabbi Aryeh Kaplan in his book the ['**Sefer Yetzirah – The Book of Formation'** -** in Theory and Practice];

'the Sefer Yetzirah is without question the oldest and most mysterious of all Kabbalistic texts'.

Rabbi Kaplan goes onto explain that 'each of the trinity of texts (The Book of Formation, the Torah and the Zohar) mentioned above contain elements of each, the Zohar and the Torah are considered to be directed towards explaining the theoretical aspects of Kabbalah, that is to say the dynamics of the spiritual domain, especially the worlds of the Sephirot, souls and angels.

Meditative Kabbalah deals with the use of divine names, letter permutations and similar methods to reach higher states of consciousness. The Sefir Yetzirah is an aid to meditation but also includes magical overtones'.

There is evidence from tradition, scripture and other texts that point to the Sefir Yetzirah being either composed by or at least available to the Patriarch Abraham – who lived around 1900 years before Jesus was born.

Magical Kabbalah is closely related to the meditative Kabbalah and consists of various signs, incantations and divine names. Through these one can heal, influence or alter natural events and telekinetic or spiritual power can be effectively channelled. The particular relevance of this to Jesus will become apparent in Chapter 8.

But remember, each of these were first understood in oral form only. Only later, often much, much later, were they written down.

The Book of Formation is a short text containing approximately 2000 words. It is difficult to decipher. Generally speaking, it is not used as an aid to understanding the Torah. Instead, the Zohar generally fulfils this role, and is used as part of every-day Kabbalah.

As I explain below, with most ancient books there is some element of controversy as to the identification of the author and also the date of composition. Moreover, the versions that we have available to us today:

- Were first preserved and transmitted orally; and
- Were developed both in oral and written form - producing different versions at different times.
- The Sefer Yetzirah that we have today may not necessarily be exactly the same as that referred to in earlier times.

In the case of the dating and authorship of the Sefer Yetzirah, the conclusion reached by Rabbi Aryeh Kaplan is that there is the following evidence:

- 'Oral traditions' as to its existence and practice are alluded to in very early manuscripts (100BC). Authorship was attributed to Abraham who lived c.1900 BC.
- It is not inconceivable that it was written by or for and on behalf of Abraham. Thus, it is at the least possible that Abraham is the author.

- The first direct written reference to use of the Sefer Yetzirah is by Rabbi Yehoshua ben Chananya, a leading sage of the 1st century.
- The Talmud which in written form dates from c.200 AD contains clear references to the existence of the Sefir Yetzhirah as beginning in oral form much earlier and then reduced to writing and used by the Jewish sages.
- There are actual quotations from a version of the Sefer Yetzirah as early as the 6th century.
- The earliest known commentaries on the Sefer Yetzirah are from the 10th century.

Nevertheless, the opinions by experts in the field as to when the Seer Yetzirah was **written** (as opposed to oral) range from before 100 BC to 900 AD.

The late Professor Gershom Scholem who for 32 years was the Professor of Jewish Mysticism and Kabbalah at the Hebrew University of Jerusalem, dates the earliest written version to 100-200 AD (Gershom, Origins of the Kabbalah). These dates coincide with the time when the 'Talmud' was first reduced to writing from its prior oral tradition. Again, more of this later. Thus - the historical evidence points to the Sefir Yetzirah and indeed other secret teachings being in existence in both oral and written form – but at least in oral form - at and around the time of Jesus. This is potentially quite significant as I explain in Chapter 8.

After the Torah, the Zohar is probably the most important, if not, equally as important literary work under-pinning Kabbalah. It is written in Aramaic, which is almost certainly the language that Jesus spoke on an everyday basis. It is likely that he also spoke Hebrew (not least as a Rabbi when reading and quoting the Torah) and even Greek, the language of commerce.

Known as the 'Book of Splendor' to Kabbalists, the Zohar is derived from an oral tradition contemporaneous with the oral Torah - reaching-back in time some 2000 years before Jesus was born. Kabbalists claim that the oral version of the Zohar was committed to writing approximately 1900 years ago following the destruction of the Temple in Jerusalem in 70 AD.

This is the view of Rabbi Kaplan and a number of other biblical scholars. But this view is by no means universally accepted within academic circles. There is some dispute as to whether the Zohar was brought into being from an oral to written version by a famous Jewish Tanin and Kabbalist – Rabbi Shimon Bar Yochai (100-160 CE) - or by the 13th century Rabbi and Kabbalist Moses de Leon.

The afore mentioned Professor Gershom Scholem asserts that the Zohar was written by Rabbi Moses de Leon in the 13th century – and that it is not based on an earlier oral tradition.

In contrast, Rabbi Aryeh Kaplan's view is that it was indeed written in the 1st Century by Rabbi Shimon bar Yochai and not by Rabbi Moses de Leon. However even if Professor Gershom Scholem is correct (and I do not say he is or is not), he himself confirms that;

"there existed between the first and the third centuries, above all in the circles of talmudists, the two esoteric disciplines attested to in the Mishnah *Hagigah* 2:1, concerning the Creation, *bereshith*, and the divine chariot of Exekial 1, the Merkabah."

(Gershom Scholem, Origins of the Kabbalah – P.19)

But these esoteric 'disciplines' are based upon the visions of the prophets Isaiah and Ezekial and concern:

- The Kingdom of God or Heaven
- The throne of God
- Ascending and descending up and from the heavens
- Angels
- Fire and Light

As we shall see, each of these are matters clearly referred to in the Synoptic Gospels in relation to Jesus.

Professor Scholem contends that these disciplines did not form part of the 12th and 13th century Kabbalah, but rather had their roots at least in written form in the Talmud.

Given other writings that are attributed to Rabbi de Leon – it seems very unlikely that he was capable of writing the Zohar. In fact, he did not even claim to be the author of the Zohar. He said that he reproduced the Zohar from an original handwritten text he possessed. He said that the Zohar had been 'revealed' by Rabbi Shimon Bar Yochai 1200 years earlier and he acknowledges Rabbi Shimon as the author.

Also to be clear, Kabbalists do not claim that Rabbi Shimon Bar Yochai actually wrote the Zohar but rather that he revealed it in an oral discourse, written down by one of his disciples and his scribe - Rabbi Abba.

As I now explain, it is at least conceivable for other reasons that Rabbi Shimon bar Yochai is the author of the Zohar. He is recognized and acknowledged not just by modern Kabbalists but also mainstream Judaism as a being one of the renowned Tannaim – Hebrew תנאים ''repeaters'', ''teachers'' in the late 1st and early 2nd centuries.

The singular 'Tanna' were Rabbinic sages whose views were recorded in a Jewish set of writings called 'the Mishnah', dating from approximately 10-220 AD.

The Mishnah is the first major written redaction (setting down) of the Jewish oral traditions known as the Old Torah or Oral Law. The Mishna supplements the written, or scriptural laws found in the Torah. It presents various interpretations of selective legal traditions that had been passed down since at least Ezra (Jewish Scribe and Priest), c.450BC.

Further study of the Mishna by Jewish scholars (called Amoraim) resulted in two collections of interpretations and annotations of the Mishna called 'Gemara' or 'Talmud', which together make up what is now known as 'The Talmud'.

The root 'tanna' תנא is the Talmudic Aramaic equivalent for the Hebrew root 'shanah' שנה which is the root-word of Mishnah. The verb shannah שנה literally means ''to repeat (what one was taught)'' and used to mean ''to learn''. In other words, it means to study by repetition.

We might never know the identity of the original author of the Zohar. In the same way, we cannot know for certain the identities of the authors of the Synoptic Gospels, nor the precise date that they were written.

This is not unusual when it comes to ancient religious and spiritual texts. For example, there are parallels in one of the most well-known and powerful Chinese spiritual books – 'Tao Te Ching' ('The Way' or 'Book of the Way'). Its authorship is traditionally attributed to a man called Laozi. But the text's true authorship and the date of composition or compilation are still debated to this day. No one knows for certain.

Likewise, what we know of Buddhism was not recorded in writing (Pali Canon) when the Buddha lived but rather approximately 450 years after his death.

TRUTH

Regardless, what the Tao Te Ching, Buddhist texts, Zohar and Synoptic Gospels have in common, are insights and wisdom that are timeless and profound. In each case, it is not unreasonable to question their authorship, date of composition, and historicity, however, what 'matters' most are the truths and core teachings contained within and whether they can aid our spiritual growth.

There is a tendency to presume that if something is old and has stood the test of time that it is more valid than something more contemporary. But that does not really stand up to close scrutiny. A truth is a truth because it touches us in a way that transcends everyday information. A truth revealed today is just as valid as one that was revealed 4,000 or 2000 years ago. It would be imprudent to discount something containing a truth simply because it was said by someone today.

After all, when Moses, Rabbi Shimon and Jesus were revealing truths - it was 'today' at that time. It was then 'the Now'. [Of course it is always and only ever 'now']. What Jesus had to say was as valid on the day he said as it is today. And like today, some people 'got it' immediately and others later – some sooner than others – and of course some not at all.

In the same way, it does not necessarily matter who reveals a truth. Of course, it is likely that the revealer is a spiritually aware person at the time of the revelation – but not necessarily an overtly religious or pious person.

In Shakespeare's 'The Tragedy of Hamlet – Prince of Denmark', in Act 2 Hamlet says:

"Why, then, tis none to you, for there is nothing either good or bad, but thinking makes it so"

And in Henry IV Part I, Falstaff says:

'The better part of valour is discretion'

I remember very vividly the moment I saw and heard Falstaff deliver these lines at an RSC performance in Stratford-upon-Avon. The potency and profoundness of the words were so great, the audience gasped. So far as we know, Shakespeare was by no means an ostensibly religious or spiritual person, but what Hamlet and Falstaff amongst many other Shakespearean characters had to say are ultimately, profound truths. Thus, whilst it is tempting to do so, we should be slow to judge the revealer. After all, Jesus was criticised by the establishment and condemned to die as a criminal. Not the best of starts when it comes to claiming authority for the truth he had to reveal.

Whenever the Zohar was revealed in written form, there is no dispute by Kabbalists and main stream Orthodox Jewry that esoteric disciplines including the Sefer Yetzirah, Doctrine of the Creation, the Merkabah and the literature of the Hekhalt, in oral form ran parallel with

84

the Torah. Both the oral and written form of the Torah came into being many centuries before the birth of Jesus. In this sense, there is evidence that Kabbalah was certainly a key body of knowledge in existence before and during the time that Jesus lived in Galilee.

For our purposes, it is perhaps important to note the following factors that are not disputed by the Catholic, Anglican and Eastern Orthodox Churches, Orthodox Jewry and Kabbalists:

- The Sefer Yetzirah and the Zohar are Jewish mystical texts.
- The Sefer Yetzirah and the Zohar were written by Jews for Jews – not by Christians for Christians.
- The Sefer Yetzirah and the Zohar are not Christian texts and do not form part of Christianity – though that may change.
- The point is, that the content of these two books would not have been written by a Rabbi to educate Christians.
- The Sefer Yetzirah was originally an oral body of knowledge probably created before the birth of Jesus and possibly from the time of the Torah.
- Oral esoteric disciplines and traditions existed within Judaism a hundred years before the birth of Jesus and would in principle as a Jewish Rabbi - have been 'available' to him.
- The Sefer Yetzirah and other esoteric traditions was circulated in oral form among a limited number of highly spiritual Rabbis.

- Such traditions ('Kabbalah') were not revealed to all Rabbis and not revealed to all Jews. It was a secret body of knowledge – hidden from all but a privileged few.
- Therefore - Any references in the Synoptic Gospels attributed to Jesus that are cross-referenced in Kabbalah and/or the Sefer Yetzirah and/or the Zohar are likely to have as their source either Kabbalah and/or the Sefer Yetzirah and/or the Zohar – the tradition or an esoteric tradition.

The Age of Aquarius

Kabbalah exists today in mainstream Judaism in the same way that it has for millennia. It is known by only a limited number of initiates all of who are Rabbis and none of who are ordinary lay people.

But with thanks to the industry of The Kabbalah Centre, Kabbalah is now available to all people of any denomination or no denomination at all, with Centres in over 40 cities throughout the world. In the 1960's, The Kabbalah Centre caused a great deal of controversy not least because it translated the Zohar into English and several other languages – but primarily because it began teaching Kabbalah to anyone wishing to learn and develop their spirituality.

The moving spirits behind these decisions were Rabbi Philip S Berg and his wife Karen Berg. They both came under considerable criticism from mainstream Judaism for 'opening up' Kabbalah. It was bad enough in the eyes of their critics that they should do so to ordinary Jews, but it was seen as anathema to do so to the non-Jews – the Gentiles. The Bergs and their two children were ostracised and even physically assaulted as a result of their decision to share the secrets of what had lain hidden since the time of Moses. In short they were persecuted.

The parallels with the persecution of the early Christians by the Jewish 'Establishment' in 1st century Israel do not stop there. Rabbi Berg caused not inconsiderable controversy for his views on the failings of the modern Judaic Establishment and some core beliefs of Judaism. His teachings of Kabbalah mirror those that we saw earlier when looking at the Gospel of John.

In his Introduction to the first English translation of the Zohar, Rabbi Berg categorically asserts that: (Zohar, 1)

- The revelation event of Moses and the Torah was not limited to Jews only.

He says:

"It is unconscionable to presume that God would present the Deity of Beneficence to one nation and not others."

- Jews are not defined by birth or race but;

"by any individual who behaves in a sharing, tolerant, and sensitive manner – by definition

is a person who acts in a Godly manner with compassion for all of God's created beings. This not only includes a consciousness of human dignity, but also respect for all other Kingdoms: animal, vegetable and mineral. This was the creation of God"

Such a person is according to Rabbi Berg - a Jew. Being a Jew is nothing to do with being born to a Jewish mother.

- The cause of anti-Semitism is and always has been;

"the Judaic deity and ecclesiastical authority"

"These Jews [The Judaic Religious Establishment] were and continue to be the underlying cause of anti-Semitism...[and] were the people to become aware of why anti-Semitism exists, they would immediately reject these hateful authoritarians."

In the view of Rabbi Philip Berg if Kabbalah and the Zohar:

"became widespread, there would be no further need of intermediaries or the deity and its authority."

Rabbi Philip Berg asserts that he was inspired and urged by his teacher Rabbi Yehudi Brandwin (heir to the legacy of Rav Yehudi Ashlag) to translate the Zohar and to make the Kabbalah and the Zohar available in the public domain. According to Rabbi Berg, the Zohar predicted that Kabbalah and the Zohar would be revealed in the 'Age of Aquarius' – which is now – and would help usher in a shift in the consciousness of all humans to create a peaceful, loving, and harmonious world. Throughout its long history, there have been attempts to introduce the Zohar and Kabbalah to the world. But as Hamlet said, the time was 'out of joint'. That is until now. Now is the favourable time.

It has taken many centuries for humans to become enlightened to the possibility that the established religions and their governing institutions have been controlling their minds and behaviour for their own ends, which has consequently been hindering people in their individual spiritual quests.

The stated aim of the Kabbalah Centre is to achieve unity and peace among all people throughout the world. So far as I can see – this is a noble aim entirely consistent with the Two Commandments earlier referred to. Kabbalah is not about division and segregation. Kabbalah is about integration and oneness - of all religious persuasions and none - of all of God's creation.

In short, what Rabbi Philip Berg is saying is that regardless of nationality, culture and religious background, if you are someone who:

'behaves in a sharing, tolerant, and sensitive manner – by definition is a person who acts in a Godly manner with compassion for all of God's created beings. This not only includes a consciousness of human dignity, but also respect for all other Kingdoms: animal, vegetable and mineral'

then, you are a Jew as originally contemplated when God handed down the Torah to Moses.

As such, you are entitled to have access to the wisdom and knowledge contained within Kabbalah not by virtue of an accident of birth but rather through virtue itself.

Chapter 5 –
Jesus: What do we know?

Before we consider the core message of Jesus and the 'authority' with which he is described to have taught, it might be useful to:

- See what we know about Jesus from an historical point of view; and
- Consider the reliability of the sources that purportedly report his words and actions.

As previously mentioned in the Introduction, 'Jesus' of course was not his actual name. The name corresponds to the Greek spelling 'Iesous', from which the later Latin becomes 'Iesus', and then the English spelling Jesus. The original Aramaic name for Jesus was ישוע and both it and the Hebrew name ישוע were written and pronounced the same as 'Yeshua' (which means 'to deliver' – 'to rescue') – or what in English would be 'Joshua'.

In Israel 2000 years ago, Yeshua was a common name – much like John would be today. Even so, we cannot know with absolute certainty that Yeshua or Joshua was his given name – though it is likely to be so. Virtually all modern scholars of antiquity (not just religious scholars) agree the person we know as Jesus existed historically. He is not a mythical figure. The main source of all information relating to Jesus is found in the New Testament.

It is believed by rabbis and academics of all persuasions that there are also indirect references to Jesus in the Talmud. Jesus is not specifically mentioned by name but it is not unreasonable to suppose that the person that is alluded to in the Talmud is indeed Jesus.

Some of the references are less than complimentary. However, it should be remembered that to the Jewish establishment Jesus was not the Messiah as prophesised. To them Jesus was perceived as a nuisance.

Remember also, that the Talmud was written by the Jewish Religious Establishment – the institution that was the target of a great deal of criticism by Jesus, as I shall discuss in Chapter 10.

Outside of the New Testament and related materials, there are two main sources of independent evidence confirming the existence of Jesus and certain aspects of his life and death. The most important potential witness of Jesus' existence is Joseph ben Matthias (his original Jewish name) – known more generally to us as Flavius Josephus (his adopted Roman name) [A.D. 37/38 – sometime after 100 A.D] or 'Josephus'.

Josephus wrote two great works:

The Jewish War begun in the years following the fall of Jerusalem in A.D. 70 and the much longer *Jewish Antiquities* written ca. 93 – 94 AD.

Both books (at least in some versions) contain passages mentioning Jesus. Regrettably one of the passages is to be found (so far) only in the Old Russian or 'Slavonic' version of the *Jewish War* and is almost certainly a later inserted Christian addition when being translated from the original Latin.

In the *Jewish Antiquities* there are two references to Jesus. The shorter passage is almost certainly authentic and occurs in a context where Josephus describes the death of the procurator Festus and the appointment of Albinus as his successor in A.D 62.

While Albinus is still on his way to Palestine, the high priest Ananus the Younger convenes the Sanhedrin without the procurator's consent and has certain persons put to death.

It is in this context that Josephus writes:

"Being therefore this kind of person [i.e. a heartless Sadducee], Ananus thinking that he had a favourable opportunity because Festus had died and Albinus was still on his way, called a meeting of judges and brought into it the brother of Jesus-who-is called-Messiah, James by name' and some others. He made accusations that they transgressed the law, and he handed them over to be stoned".

James is actually the English form of the Greek 'Iakobos', Jacob. It is such a common name in Jewish society that Josephus needs some designation to specify which Jacob/James he is talking about. He does not seem to know James' pedigree (i.e. James son of Joseph) and so uses his brother Jesus (Joshua) as his point of reference.

What is also interesting about this passage is that neither the New Testament nor the early Christian writers spoke of James (of Jerusalem) in a matter of fact way as 'the brother of Jesus', but rather as we might expect, as 'the brother of the Saviour' or 'the brother of the Lord'. It is reasonable to deduce therefore, that this passage of Josephus is not likely to have come from a Christian hand.

There is also a second passage that after much scholarly debate almost certainly contains at least some element of later Christian interloping. But at its core there is some reasonable and proper basis to allow that at least the following elements of the passage is from Josephus alone:

"At this time there appeared Jesus, a wise man. For he was a doer of startling deeds, a teacher of people who receive the truth with pleasure. And he gained a following among many Jews and among many of Greek origin. And when Pilate, because of an accusation made by leading men among us, condemned him to the cross, those who had loved him previously did not cease to do so. And up until this very day the tribe of Christians (named after him) has not died out."

There are other sources of independent material pointing to the existence of Jesus and his life.

The Roman historian Tacitus wrote as the last great work of his life the *Annals*, in which he intended to cover the history of Rome from AD 14 to 66. Some of the books of the *Annals* have been lost. One of the gaps in the Annals occurs during the treatment of AD 29 with the narrative resuming in AD 32 - this of course being the likely period of Jesus's ministry as recorded in the New Testament. It is possible and speculated that this text may be found hidden in the Vatican library in Rome.

There is however, a short indirect reference to Jesus when Tacitus deals with the great fire of Rome under Nero.

Tacitus says that Nero blamed the fire on the Christians;

"Therefore to squelch the rumour, Nero created scapegoats and subjected to the most refined tortures those whom the common people called 'Christians' [a group] hated for their abominable crimes. Their name comes from 'Christ', who, during the reign of Tiberius, had been executed by the procurator Pontius Pilate. Suppressed for the moment, the deadly superstition broke out again, not only in Judea, the land which originated this evil, but also in the city of Rome, where all sorts of horrendous and shameful practices from every part of the world converge and are fervently cultivated."

Now content that Jesus did in fact roam the Earth, we can now turn to what he said and did - albeit with some caution and qualification.

Caution

So far as we are aware, save for one instance where Jesus is recorded as writing something on the ground [John 8:6-8], Jesus did not write or instruct anyone to write of what he taught. Thus, we cannot know with absolute certainty all that Jesus said or did. Indeed, we cannot know with absolute certainty very much about Jesus – especially when it comes to what he said. We can of course believe anything we want, but that will not make it true.

Whilst it is possible - it is extremely unlikely that what is attributed as being the words of Jesus are verbatim what he said. At best, they are:

- A very close record of a prior oral tradition
- That recited the purport or 'gist' and/or
- Generally accepted understanding of what Jesus had said and sought to convey.

This is not a controversial position. Mainstream Christian scholars agree with what I am saying here.

As previously noted, the primary source of what is claimed Jesus said and did is in the New Testament, in particular the Synoptic Gospels of Matthew, Mark and Luke. These are not meant to be 'historical' documents in the way that we understand a history book today. They are statements of an already existing set of beliefs. To an objective observer they might reasonably be considered either wholly or in part as self-serving. In fact, the earliest written documents concerning Jesus and his life are the Acts of the Apostles and the letters of St. Paul to the various 'churches' Paul visited during his lifetime. Some of these documents concerning Jesus and his life were written about 20 years after Jesus' crucifixion – much closer in time than the four Gospels.

But these documents save in respect of one or two exceptions, do not record the sayings of Jesus – or the words he used when he was teaching. Almost certainly the author(s) of the Acts and the various letters would have been familiar with the oral version of the Gospels – which were subsequently then put into writing. The oral accounts of Jesus were the backdrop against which the Acts and letters of St Paul and others were written. To learn what the followers of Jesus say he taught and what his 'message' was, we have to turn to the Synoptic Gospels – and in doing so, must consider what is recorded with some caution and reservation.

Here is why one must proceed with some caution:

- Our main sources for what Jesus said and did from a historical basis, are the three Synoptic Gospels books of the Gospel of which two (Matthew and Luke) are largely a re-working of Mark.

- These books were based on a prior oral tradition in Aramaic; the story being at least 30 years old – during which time there was at least the possibility and more probably a likelihood of change.
- We do not know who the actual authors were. Who was Mark? It is the Gospel according to Mark. Was he the author? There is no scholarly agreement on this matter.
- The original handwritten versions of the Gospels and indeed any part of the New Testament no longer exist. We only have copies of copies.
- The earliest fragment (the size of a credit card) of any part of the New Testament is part of the Gospel of John dating from c.125AD.
- The earliest copies of most but not all the New Testament Gospels and writings dates are contained in various fragments from c.160AD.
- The earliest extant complete copy of the contents of the New Testament is from the 3rd Century.
- Our source materials are copies of what was an oral tradition in one language (Aramaic), translated into Greek and/or then to Latin – and finally (for us) to English, and of course many other languages.

Moreover, the problem and impact of translation should not be underestimated. In the case of an English New Testament such as the New Standard **Revised** Edition [my emphasis] – the title says it all – well nearly all.

In the Introduction to the Reader of the New Standard Revised Edition, the Editors not so much acknowledge as warn:

"No translation of the Bible is perfect...The Bible carries its full message...to all persons and communities who read it so that they may discern and understand what God is saying to them. That message must not be disguised in phrases that are no longer clear, or hidden under words that have changed or lost their meaning: it must be presented in language that is direct and plain and meaningful to people today."

But there are more issues than the meaning of words. It is worth reading the 'Introduction to the Reader' as it highlights the many choices that the Editors of the New Standard Revised Edition faced. These include decisions as to which of different versions of the same texts should be used, accounting for advances in the discovery and interpretation of documents in Semitic languages, altering vowels from a Masoretic text:

"where a probable convincing reading can be assumed by using different vowels."

Even when all of this scholarly work is done it should be remembered that what they are translating for us is several steps removed from when Jesus actually spoke. Despite all of these issues, I think it is possible to discern the central messages of Jesus and to see their connection and source within Kabbalah.

Authority

It is helpful to understand the ministry of Jesus in the religious context of 1st century Israel. Like Christianity and Judaism today, there were several factions of Judaism in existence contemporary to Jesus. The New Testament itself refers to Pharisees but there were also the sects known as Sadducees and Essenes. Early Christians shared several beliefs of the Pharisees such as resurrection, retribution in the next world and angels. Some scholars believe that Jesus was a Pharisee.

The Pharisees themselves were divided into two main schools of thought. Firstly - the House of Hillel which had been founded by the eminent Tanna, Hillel the Elder, and secondly, the House of Shammai. Hillel the Elder was a famous Jewish religious leader and is reckoned to be one of the most important figures in Jewish history. He is associated with the development of the Mishnah and the Talmud and was the founder of the House of Hillel school for Tannaim. He was known for his teaching the Spirit of the Law in contrast to Shammai whose teachings emphasised adherence to the strict Letter of the Law. But it is by no means entirely clear as to what Hillel himself said and what his followers subsequently attributed to him. The same should be said of Jesus and his followers.

Likewise, the dates of Hillel's birth and death cannot be known for certain but it is thought that he lived in Jerusalem from c.30 BC and died there around 10 AD. Given the age gap, it seems unlikely that Jesus would have had direct contact with Hillel but it is at least possible that he was aware of Hillel's teachings. Certainly, some of the things that Jesus is reported as saying are consistent with Hillel's teaching – but there again, that is not entirely surprising given that Hillel was really promulgating main stream Judaism as found in the Torah.

Jesus seems to direct criticisms of hypocrisy on several occasions to those who adhere to the strict letter of the Law. It may be that such criticisms are aimed at the stricter members of the House of Shammai – and also the Sadducees. The Sadducees were a powerful group of Law observant Jews in Jerusalem at the time of Jesus. They accepted the written Law only and held beliefs different to the Pharisees on subjects such as an afterlife, resurrection of the body, angels and spirits.

Inevitably, there has also been conjecture that Jesus was an Essene – another one of the main groups of the time. The Essenes were apocalyptic ascetics and a community of them lived at Khirbet Qumran in the eastern Judean Desert, the modern West bank. It is from this community that the Dead Sea Scrolls originate. These scrolls comprise of more than 900 different texts and the current consensus is that they date from at least the third century BC and the first century AD.

As Jewish apocalyptics, they believed that there are two eras of history. The first is the current one which is ruled over by evil and the second is a world to come to be ruled over by God. There is speculation (and it is no

101

more than that) that Jesus may have been part of the Essene community. It should however be noted that there is no direct reference to Jesus in the Scrolls that have been released and/or published to date. There is no direct reference in the New Testament to Jesus being part of any community – Essene or otherwise. Qumran is quite a distance from Galilee and the towns and villages where Jesus is reported as preaching. It seems likely that if he was living and preaching in or around Qumran there would be some mention of it in the New Testament. There is not.

Indeed, it seems unlikely that Jesus was a Pharisee or an Essene or had a belief system that was anything different from traditional Judaism as found in the Torah. But - as I previously noted, there was something that marked him out as being unique and different.

On several occasions the Gospels report how Jesus speaks with an 'authority' which his listeners declared to be perplexing and yet astounding. These reports point to both something about how he presents himself – his 'vibe' or 'energy' and something that he knows that others do not.

We are told at a very early stage of the Synoptic Gospels what Jesus began to teach:

"Jesus came to Galilee, proclaiming the good news of God, saying, ''The time is fulfilled, and the Kingdom of God has come near, repent, and believe in the good news.''

[Mark 1 :15]

Likewise, Matthew repeated the same point:

"From that time Jesus began to proclaim, 'Repent, for the Kingdom of God has come near'."

[Mathew 4:17]

On the face of it, this is a very succinct and simple message. It comprises of three elements:

1. The Kingdom of God.
2. Repent to find the Kingdom.
3. The Kingdom is near.

This message is at the very heart of the teaching of Jesus. It may be simple but further explanation may be required to make the full nature and extent of its implications understood to all. Much of the Synoptic Gospels is about those further explanations.

It is to these elements of what Jesus began to preach that I now turn. For as I shall show, these elements are the core message of Jesus and Kabbalah.

Chapter 6 –
Metanoia

Psychosis

"A severe mental disorder in which thought and emotions are so impaired that contact is lost with external reality"

(Oxford English Dictionary)

The Pope recently observed that 'the world is at war' (Catholic Herald, 2016). In fact, it always has been. It is the very nature of the human condition to find itself to be in a state of conflict, chaos – what Buddhists call 'Dukkha' - that is to say 'suffering'. How often have we each of us said 'the world is mad' – without realising that in medical terms – this is actually correct?

Humans appear to have a strong propensity to be psychotic. More accurately put – by far and the majority of Humans at least some of the time - live in and demonstrate a mental attitude and behaviour consistent with

'A severe mental disorder in which thought and emotions are so impaired that contact is lost with external reality'

- i.e. psychotic behaviour.

104

This accurate assertion is important because the psychosis is not always everywhere and experienced by everyone – and this means that there are lucid periods for some if not all people at some time. If humans can be sane, why do they choose not to be? If there are lucid periods – then there is the opportunity for change for everyone – during the lucid periods. There has never been a time when humans have not fought either openly or covertly against their rulers and/or their neighbours – and often both - simultaneously.

The Torah mirrors this position throughout its many books. There are numerous reports of every heinous crime imaginable. Murder, rape, torture, theft and more. Such is the degenerate behaviour of humankind that on several occasions God threatens to wipe out the entire human race. In the intervening period very little has changed. On any day at anytime, anywhere in the world - just browse the Internet, TV News Channels and Newspapers and you will see exactly what I mean.

But somehow the current state of conflict in each and every country feels different from what has come before. Somehow, there is a burgeoning awareness by a greater and increasing number of people that the conflicts our leaders commit us to are not underpinned by a sense of proper purpose – an aim to achieve a worthy or just outcome. Often, we are asked to go to war (whether economically or militarily) against people that:

- We had probably wronged in the first place; or
- We had supported whilst it was convenient – and then withdrew the support
- We had provided with arms

But of course, when I say 'we' I mean those politicians and leaders that act in our name. The so-called 'War on Terror' and the attempt to impose 'Democracy' have failed in all of the countries where it was imposed or attempts were made to impose it.

But more importantly, the very concept of Democracy – at least as it has been or is being practiced - is itself being challenged from within those countries that advocate it – and seek to insist on its singular correctness.

Consider even just a few landmark events of 2016 and 2017, for instance, the 'Trump/Clinton' Presidential elections in the United States or 'Brexit', whereby the United Kingdom voted to leave the European Union.

The fight against Democracy and the institutions of Democracy is from both without and within. That fight has come to resemble and reflect the inner conflict that we all have. We are torn in the effort to find balance between the spiritual and material aspects of our lives. People are sick of the 'establishment' and the way that things have been done and continue to be done – ostensibly in our name. People are looking for change – but are looking in the wrong place. The 'system' that has caused the disease cannot cure it. There needs to a different approach.

People are at last realising the unfairness of the market approach to living - an approach that by its very nature means there are always going to be 'winners' and 'losers'. There are the exploiters and exploited. There are more and more 'losers' even from the ranks of the former 'winners'; there is a groundswell of dissatisfaction at a profound level. But what can we do about that?

The desire for something more

People are asking themselves - 'Is this all there is to life? I am born, go to school, then to work, and then to die? And all the while living in a near constant state of, at best, background anxiety, at worse, outright fear and depression?'. No wonder there is conflict. Most of us live our lives in fear to a varying degree and feel threatened from all angles. Even when things are 'going well', the feeling of non-fear does not seem to last long. Why does any sense of 'achievement' give only a temporary relief? Surely there is more to Life than this!

There is!

The good news - is that it is possible to live without fear. It is possible to live with a feeling of deep and lasting happiness. It is available to you and indeed all of us. The first critical step towards such happiness begins once you recognize the unhappiness; the fear and the anxiety that you endure.

First you need to see and accept that there is a problem. It is already progress when you realize that you are not happy. You have made a shift to a higher level in your consciousness, in your spiritual awareness.

The next step is to find out what to look for and where and how to look. Every day now, for many people including you - the awakening is greater and more profound. In time, it will come to be the norm.

In organised religion, desire is often portrayed as a bad thing – something to give up. But desire is both a catalyst and an essential ingredient for change. The challenge with desire is to control the direction in which it is targeted. Is it a desire for spiritual growth and connection to God and all creation – or for purely selfish reasons?

A great many people desire changes to the political landscape. There is a sense of injustice being inflicted upon them and others.

But on close examination, political change is only on the surface of the sense of unease. The political systems are a manifestation of the inner aspect of each person. If you bother to vote - you get what the majority vote for – what the majority stand for.

This is true of the established 'Churches' and organized religion also. How many times in recent years have we seen that the human element of organised religion – the very people that we had been told to look to as examples – have failed to reach the mark. When this happens we should be slow to judge the people concerned, but rather take it as a sign that responsibility for our happiness does not lie with those people or anybody else – but in ourselves. We must take control of our own happiness.

Lasting and meaningful change cannot come at the level of consciousness that has created the problems we now all face. It can only come from a different and higher consciousness. The change has to first start from within each person – within YOU – not anybody else.

We each of us have to take responsibility for our own thoughts, words and actions. Taking personal responsibility is a core teaching of Jesus and Kabbalah.

Amazingly - it is a feature of the apparently worsening state of the material world – the world of form, the physical world - that there is a concomitant increase in the search for meaning and spiritual consciousness. I am not alone in sensing a spiritual shift - a change of direction from material to spiritual. It is what the New Testament calls 'metanoia' – a word that has been mistranslated and misunderstood by the Christian Churches with regrettable consequences.

Metanoia means a total change in outlook on how to live and experience life. It is a shift from the almost exclusive pursuit of the left column to the primary (not exclusive) pursuit of the goals listed in the right column in Chapter 2.

It is clear that the change in level of consciousness, the 'metanoia', can only come from within YOU and in this way the internal will give rise to the external changes you seek, and indeed we all seek. The implications of this are discussed in much more detail later in this chapter.

It is worth noting that both Jesus and Kabbalah do not invite people to change other people – they both invite YOU to examine you – and then for you to respond – of course only if YOU wish to. You have the opportunity and power within you – to change you by the choices you make. A change in your choices will give rise to a change in how you think, speak and act. In turn this will make all the difference in creating a better world for you – and with that, the world of everyone and everything that you come into contact with.

How can you do that? Where is the answer? Do you take, as Morpheus in the Matrix invited Neo, the red pill or the blue pill?

It is within your power to enter into a state of being that is a life without fear, a life of joy and deep and lasting happiness. It is the hidden treasure – waiting to be discovered. Jesus called that state of being 'the Kingdom of God' or the Kingdom of Heaven'. Kabbalah calls it 'the Light'. Both allude to a source of deep and lasting happiness. The light may be hidden beneath a number of layers. But as you remove each layer, the Light increases and eventually will become so intense and so widespread that it will envelop and reflect off you.

How do I find that state of being – the Light, the hidden treasure? The answer is closer than you think. It is within your reach. But to grasp it, you must do one thing. Choose to focus on what really matters.

As I previously noted, the Gospel according to Mark is the closest in time to the life of Jesus to be written.

In Mark, 1:14 provides us with Jesus's **first spoken words** and they proclaim what Jesus was preaching:

Jesus came to Galilee, proclaiming the good news of God, and saying,

> **"The time is fulfilled, and the Kingdom of God has come near; <u>repent</u>, and believe in the good news."**

[Mark 1:14]

The first three chapters of Matthew are spent in providing a genealogy of Jesus, details of his birth and the meeting between John the Baptist and Jesus – his cousin.

In Chapter 4 of Matthew, we read that following the arrest of John the Baptist Jesus

"withdrew to Galilee... and <u>from that time</u> Jesus began to proclaim"

"'Repent, for the Kingdom of heaven has come near'".

Luke approaches the matter in a slightly different way. Like Matthew, the first part of his gospel deals with the birth, the first couple of years of Jesus's childhood – and his meeting with John the Baptist. In fact, there are significant differences in what Matthew and Luke say on these topics but they are not really relevant to our discussion here.

Following the tests and temptations of Satan in the desert Luke 4:18 says:

"Then filled with the power of the Spirit, [Jesus] returned to Galilee, and a report of him spread through all surrounding country. He began to teach in their synagogues and was praised by everyone."

What Luke describes next is that Jesus went to the synagogue in his home town of Nazareth;

"[Jesus] stood up to read, and the scroll of the prophet Isaiah was given to him. He unrolled the scroll and found the place where it was written:

''The Spirit of the Lord is upon me, because he has anointed me to bring good news to the poor. He has sent me to proclaim release to the captives and

recovery of sight to the blind, to let the oppressed go free, to proclaim the year of the Lord's favour''.

And he rolled up the scroll, gave it back to the attendant, and sat down...he began to say to them;

''Today this scripture is fulfilled in your hearing.''

What scripture? The passage that Jesus is quoting from is a passage from the prophet Isaiah 61:1.

"The spirit of the Lord God is upon me, because the Lord has anointed me; he has sent me to bring the good news to the oppressed, to bind up the broken hearted, to proclaim the liberty to the captives, and release to the prisoners; to proclaim the year of the Lord's favour"

Note that Jesus is reported by Luke as rolling up the scriptures after this particular passage. In fact, Isaiah 61 goes on for much longer – in fact ten (10) more verses.

Indeed, the Book of Isaiah is quite a large book with sixty six (66) chapters. If as Luke claims, Jesus really did read from the scroll and from Isaiah in particular, he had quite a lot to choose from - including passages also from Isaiah that were subsequently used by Christian theologians to support their belief that Jesus was the Messiah as prophesied by Isaiah. But apparently on this occasion Jesus did not read aloud those passages to this audience.

It is helpful to remember that Isaiah lived around 600 years before Jesus was born and that a prophet was not someone that foretold the future.

The English word *prophet* comes from the Greek word προφήτης *profétés* meaning, advocate or speaker.

A **prophet** is an individual who has claimed to have been contacted by the supernatural or divine; speaking for them and serving as an intermediary with humanity. Usually a prophet will deliver a new insight or an affirmation of an original, longstanding insight – in each case disclosed by God.

In Judaism, a person was examined and tested by the Sanhedrin to establish the person's credentials as a prophet. The Book of Isaiah is written in the present tense, first person singular - as though God himself is speaking to the people of Israel.

The prophecy is an unfolding and reminder of God's law and the consequences of adhering to it (good) and not adhering to it (bad) and the need to get back to it. Had Jesus wanted to tell everyone that he is the Messiah, then he might have read and declared fulfilment in him of either of the following passages from Isaiah and/or other prophets in the Hebrew Bible.

However, he did not. These passages were applied to him by some of the early Christians. Let me repeat – Jesus is not reported as saying these things about himself.

[Isaiah 9:1-2]

The people that walked in darkness have seen a great
light: they that dwell in the land of the shadow of
death, upon them hath the light shined.
Thou hast multiplied the nation, and not increased
the joy: they joy before thee according to the joy in
harvest, and as men rejoice when they divide the
spoil.
For thou hast broken the yoke of his burden, and the
staff of his shoulder, the rod of his oppressor, as in
the day of Midian.
For every battle of the warrior is with confused noise,
and garments rolled in blood; but this shall be with
burning and fuel of fire.
For unto us a child is born, unto us a son is given:
and the government shall be upon his shoulder: and
his name shall be called Wonderful, Counsellor, The
mighty God, The everlasting Father, The Prince of
Peace.
Of the increase of his government and peace there
shall be no end, upon the throne of David, and upon
his Kingdom, to order it, and to establish it with
judgment and with justice from henceforth even for
ever. The zeal of the LORD of hosts will perform this.

Or:

[Isaiah 53:2]

Who hath believed our report? and to whom is the
arm of the LORD revealed?
For he shall grow up before him as a tender plant,
and as a root out of a dry ground: he hath no form
nor comeliness; and when we shall see him, there is
no beauty that we should desire him.
He is despised and rejected of men; a man of sorrows,
and acquainted with grief: and we hid as it were our
faces from him; he was despised, and we esteemed
him not.
Surely he hath borne our griefs, and carried our
sorrows: yet we did esteem him stricken, smitten of
God, and afflicted.
But he was wounded for our transgressions, he was
bruised for our iniquities: the chastisement of our
peace was upon him; and with his stripes we are
healed.
All we like sheep have gone astray; we have turned
every one to his own way; and the LORD hath laid on
him the iniquity of us all.
He was oppressed, and he was afflicted, yet he opened
not his mouth: he is brought as a lamb to the
slaughter, and as a sheep before her shearers is
dumb, so he openeth not his mouth.
He was taken from prison and from judgment: and
who shall declare his generation? for he was cut off
out of the land of the living: for the transgression of
my people was he stricken.
And he made his grave with the wicked, and with the
rich in his death; because he had done no violence,
neither was any deceit in his mouth.
Yet it pleased the LORD to bruise him; he hath put

him to grief: when thou shalt make his soul an offering for sin, he shall see his seed, he shall prolong his days, and the pleasure of the LORD shall prosper in his hand.

He shall see of the travail of his soul, and shall be satisfied: by his knowledge shall my righteous servant justify many; for he shall bear their iniquities.

Therefore will I divide him a portion with the great, and he shall divide the spoil with the strong; because he hath poured out his soul unto death: and he was numbered with the transgressors; and he bare the sin of many, and made intercession for the transgressors.

It seems to me to be highly significant that what Luke does not report is Jesus reading from either of these or any other passages in Isaiah (or other books in the Torah) that point to Jesus fulfilling the prophecy of and concerning a Messiah. Indeed, nowhere in the Synoptic Gospels does Jesus claim (from his reported words) to be a Messiah or especially the Messiah.

Luke is categorically reporting that Jesus declares himself to be the person that Isaiah prophesied would **bring the good news**. In other words Luke is writing that Jesus declares himself to be a messenger – a prophet.

He reports the **"time is fulfilled"** aspect of what Mark says Jesus began preaching. That is to say:

> **"The time is fulfilled, and the Kingdom of God has come near; repent, and believe in the good news'."**

What is fulfilled? The underline delivery of the good news. What has come near – the Kingdom of God.

The word "Fulfil" or an equivalent occurs in the following New Testament books:

New Testament Books	References for 'fulfil'
Matthew	1:22; 2:15, 17, 23; 4:14; 8:17; 12:17; 13:14, 35; 17:11; 21:4; 26:54, 56; 27:9.
Mark	13:4; 14:49; 15:28.
Luke	1:20, 23; 2:6, 22; 4:21; 9:31, 51; 12:50; 18:31; 21:22, 24; 22:16, 37; 24:44.
John	12:38; 13:18; 15:25; 17:12; 18:9,32; 19:24, 28, 36.
Acts	1:16; 2:1; 3:18; 13:27,29; 15:15, 24:27.
Romans	8:4; 15:19.
Timothy	4:17.
James	2:23.
Revelation	17:17.

The word "fulfil" is derived from the Aramaic דמלא D'MALA, Hebrew מלא MALEY, or the Greek πληρώ PLEROO. It means to fill full, accomplish, carry out or to bring to realization, to perform or do, as in a person's duty; or to obey or follow the Commandments, as in satisfying the Commandments by obeying them.

In the context of what Jesus is reported by Luke as saying as I quote above, the word 'fulfilled' clearly means that the prophesy is being realized in the person of Jesus. He is the person who was prophesised to deliver the good news. There is no other reasonable construction of what Luke records.

When Jesus speaks of the Kingdom of God having come near the Hebrew word he uses is אגיזין **eggizein.**

It has been said that the best possible translation of the verb **eggizein** is probably "come near" or "drawn near" (John P. Meir -, A Marginal Jew (Vol II). There have been different understandings as to what this is trying to convey. One possibility is that the Kingdom has come – it is here already – near at hand. The other is that the Kingdom is making itself felt but it has not fully arrived or materialized. It is yet to materialize. It requires something to be done.

As I will explain during the course of the book – both are correct.

Repentance & Sin

As we have seen, the first words that Jesus is reported as saying - in the Gospel that was written closest in time to his life (i.e. Mark) is:

"The time is fulfilled, and the Kingdom of God has come near; <u>repent,</u> and believe in the good news'."

[My emphasis]

Put another way – Jesus is saying:

- I am fulfilling the prophecy of Isaiah – that is – I am the person bringing the good news
- The good news is that the Kingdom has drawn near
- Repent - and you too will enter the Kingdom.

This might be shortened still further to:

- The Kingdom is within your grasp – now - here on earth.
- Adjust your way of looking at life and the Kingdom is available to you.

As will be discussed in this chapter, what Jesus really meant by the word that is translated as 'repent' is not what the established Christian Churches have taught for the past two thousand years. This has been to our detriment.

When looked at it in the context of the Synoptic Gospels as a whole, it seems to me to be obvious that the central message or messages that Jesus was preaching is captured in these words;

"i. The time is fulfilled, <u>and</u> ii. the Kingdom of God iii. has come near; iv. repent, <u>and</u> v. believe in the good news'."

[Mark 1:14]

I invite you to reflect upon these points namely:

Firstly, these are the first words that Jesus is said to have spoken concerning his teaching.

Secondly, they convey what Jesus 'began to preach'. So this is what his purpose was. This is the message that he is to deliver.

Thirdly, Jesus is not reported as beginning to preach (anything) else.

In these circumstances, we should look at them carefully.

Repentance – [Greek μετάνοια] Metanoia.

The call to 'repent' is clearly related to the Kingdom of God. In looking at what is meant by 'repent' we get a better idea of the message that Jesus was trying to impart – and with it, the connection to Kabbalah.

There cannot be any room for reasonable doubt that Jesus's main call to action is to 'repent'. If what I have already quoted is insufficient, then look closer at what Jesus is said to have instructed his disciples to preach and what we are told they did:

"Then he went among the villages teaching. He called the twelve and began to send them out two by two, and gave them authority over the unclean spirits. He ordered them to take nothing for their journey except a staff; no bread, no bag, no money in their belts, but to wear sandals and to put on two tunics. He said to them, ''Wherever you enter a house, stay there until you leave the place. If any place will not welcome you and they refuse to hear you, as you leave, shake off the dust that is on your feet as a testimony against them.

So they went out and proclaimed that all should repent"

[Mark 6:12]

The instructions are quite detailed. It is obvious that the disciples were not instructed to preach anything else. The message that they were instructed to preach was very simple:

all should repent'

But what does this mean?

The word repent is a translation of the Greek μετάνοια metanoia.

What Mark actually writes is that Jesus said:

'The time is fulfilled, and the Kingdom of God has come near; μετάνοια _metanoia_ and believe in the good news'.''

And

'They went out and proclaimed that all should μετάνοια _metanoia_'

That Greek word 'metanoia' has for two thousand years been translated as the verb 'repent' which according to the Oxford English Dictionary means to 'Feel or express sincere regret or remorse about one's wrongdoing or sin'.

The etymology of the word 'repent' is:

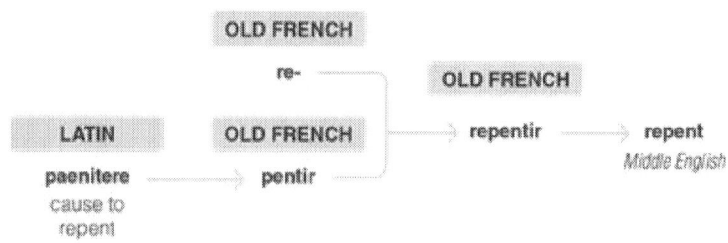

In short repent means to feel regret or sorrow. Metanoia is not just that.

Metanoia is much more than that.

In Judaism and in Kabbalah there is a call for us all to repent of our errors or 'sins' at a profound level. Kabbalah considers repentance to come about through a deep reflection on the error and to regret it with a heart-felt sincerity, to the extent that it might bring one to tears and the need to convey the regret to the person or persons you have mistreated.

Probably one of - if not - the most used (more than 100 times in the Bible) and misunderstood words in Christianity, 'repentance' and 'repent' have come to be understood by Christians as reviewing specific thoughts, words and actions and feeling contrition, sorrow or regret for past 'wrongs'. In this context, the 'wrong' being a 'sin'. If you repent of your sin(s), you acknowledge the sin and repent – feel contrite or sorry – for what you have said or done – and resolve not to repeat it.

But this is not what the Greek metanoia means. This word 'metanoia' is primarily quite literally an 'after (meta) thought (nous meaning mind)' as distinct from a 'former thought'. In Classical Greek, metanoia meant changing one's mind about someone or something. Metanoia is the act of turning/changing the direction of your thoughts or your consciousness around – or about face – from how you thought before to a new (after) thought. It imputes a change of mind and heart.

In the context of what Jesus is preaching it is a call to a complete change of, a complete shift in or a movement towards what we would call today - 'consciousness'.

According to the Oxford English Dictionary 'consciousness' means:

"a person's awareness or perception of something".

In short – it is if necessary a complete change in the way that you look at things. It is a necessary shift of where our thoughts and energy should be directed. A new outlook, a volte-face.
I consulted with Dr Maria Stamatopoulou, an Oxford University Lecturer in Classical Art & Archaeology and native Greek speaker, who confirmed that the Greek word metanoia has been translated in Christian scriptures as 'repent' but 'metanoia' both in Classical Greek and in Modern Greek imparts more than a concept of a recognition of deep regret and a deep heart felt sorrow. It means a change in direction of thought that includes regret and deep sorrow but additionally a commitment towards moving in a totally different direction to avoid repetition. She said;

"It is a total shift in consciousness. A complete change in your outlook on life".

The doctrine of repentance in the Torah is likewise a call to make a radical turn from one way of life to another. The repentance (*metanoia*) called for is a summons to a personal, absolute and ultimate unconditional all-embracing acknowledgement of the Creator and Creation. The metanoia called for throughout the Torah is a summons to obey the primary and most important commandment namely;

"Hear, O Israel: The Lord our God is alone. You shall love the Lord your God with all your heart, <u>and</u> with all your soul, <u>and</u> with all your might"

(Deuteronomy, 6:4-5)

You do not feel regret for wrongs in order to entirely 'love God'. That is not enough. Repentance is only a part of it - albeit an important part. Understanding what it means to love God and who or what we mean when we say God is in fact at the very heart of what Jesus and Kabbalah teach.

Of course, the process of changing your way of looking at things will give rise to an acknowledgment, regret and sorrow for past words and deeds – and even a resolve not to repeat. But those are outcomes derived from the metanoia – not the metanoia itself.

Jesus's message is therefore a call to a 180-degree change of direction – a turnaround - from the way we look at and act in the world now to another way. The repeated use of the word 'and' as I have underlined above emphasizes this shift. It is a call to love God with everything you possess. That is to say:

All of your heart; **and**
All of your soul; **and**
All of your might.
That is pretty much everything you have.

Jesus was saying the good news is that by changing our level of consciousness - by turning our attention entirely towards the <u>Kingdom</u>, we can and will draw closer to the <u>Kingdom</u> now. And what is the <u>Kingdom</u>? At one level it is a state of being.

But as we shall see in due course, in Kabbalah it can be understood as referring to something quite specific. As day follows night, the greater the shift of concentration towards the Kingdom the greater the awareness arises of past wrongs and failings, which in turn gives rise to deep and heartfelt regret and sorrow for past thoughts, words and deed.

The fundamental change in direction envisaged by metanoia is also at the heart of Kabbalah.

In modern Kabbalah, a distinction is drawn between what it calls on the one hand 'the 1%' and on the other, 'the 99%'.

The 1% is the level of consciousness that many people live in most of the time. It is a level of consciousness that contains and is driven by the ego – the part of the human consciousness that desires things only for itself. It is the ego that out of fear for its survival acts selfishly and violently. It is the ego that gives rise to the fear and resulting chaos that we see in the world around us. It is the cause of psychosis.

In contrast, the 99% is where the higher levels of consciousness can be found and where the ego is reduced at each level of consciousness to the point of extinction. This 99% is where the Light that emanates from God can be found and with it deep and lasting peace and happiness.

Kabbalah recognises that we each of us have desires and that the challenge for each of us is to redirect those desires away from an egoic, selfish direction – the 1% - towards the Light - the 99% - and in consequence the good of ourselves and our neighbours.

The teachings of Kabbalah are about the need to take personal responsibility for change and how to change one's attention from the 1% to the 99%. A shift from the self, to the Light.

The terms used by Jesus and modern Kabbalah differ - but the underlying principles do not. Another way of expressing this is to say that the metanoia, the call to action of Kabbalah, is to move from the self to others:

Metanoia

From	To
1%	99%
Ego (desire for self)	Non Ego (desire for others)
Inward looking	Outreaching to others
Selfishness	Loving your neighbor
Fear	Happiness
Darkness	Light
Hell	Heaven
Dharma (Chaos)	Order
Ignorance	Consciousness
Ways of the world	Kingdom (of God)
Material	Spiritual

The concept of metanoia is linked directly with the word 'sin' – another word that has been mistranslated and misunderstood almost throughout the history of Christianity. The word 'sin' has come to mean a transgression of God's commandments. In one sense this is not incorrect but it does not fully capture what was intended by the original Hebrew word which is 'hata' חטא.

The word 'hata' is derived from archery and literally means, 'missing the gold at the centre of a target but still hitting the target', i.e. error. Archers call not hitting the target at all a 'miss'. Sin therefore is not hitting the centre target (i.e. missing the mark) or missing the centre of what you are aiming for. So an adjustment in direction would then hit the mark. In this way, if one is missing the mark, then the process of metanoia (change of direction of thought) would bring the target (God and Kingdom) into view.

The target is of course the Kingdom of God – that is what you should be aiming towards and looking to meet – not of course with an arrow – but with your whole being.

It really is that simple.

That process of metanoia is a process of change that arises by looking and responding to people and circumstances, not from the way of the world, the ego, but from God's view – from the Light – the 99%.

Life will always present people and events that challenge us and it is how we respond to those challenges that indicate the extent to which we have turned around and live in the Kingdom – under God's dominion or rule. Are we on target or off target?

In Chapter 5 of the Gospel of Matthew, we read what are commonly known as 'the Beatitudes' and some additional teachings on the priority to be given to spiritual pursuits rather than earthly pursuits.

The term *beatitude* comes from the Latin noun *beātitūdō* which means "happiness".

The Gospel of Luke (Chapter 6) reports a similar event and teachings but not quite as comprehensively as Matthew.

The 'Beatitudes' do not appear in the Gospel of Mark at all.

Here is what Jesus is reported as saying on the question of spiritual pursuit. It gives a clear direction as to where this shift of attention should be directed and why:

"Do not store up for yourselves treasures on earth, where moth and rust consume and where thieves break in and steal; but <u>store up for yourselves treasures in heaven,</u> where neither moth nor rust consumes and where thieves do not break in and steal.

For where your treasure is, there your heart will be also.

Serving Two Masters

"No one can serve two masters; for a slave will either hate the one and love the other, or be devoted to the one and despise the other. <u>You cannot serve God and wealth.</u>

Do Not Worry

"Therefore I tell you, do not worry about your life, what you will eat or what you will drink, or about your body, what you will wear.

Is not life more than food, and the body more than clothing? Look at the birds of the air; they neither sow nor reap nor gather into barns, and yet your heavenly Father feeds them.

Are you not of more value than they? And can any of you by worrying add a single hour to your span of life? And why do you worry about clothing? Consider the lilies of the field, how they grow; they neither toil nor spin, yet I tell you, even Solomon in all his glory was not clothed like one of these.

But if God so clothes the grass of the field, which is alive today and tomorrow is thrown into the oven, will he not much more clothe you - you of little faith?

Therefore, do not worry, saying, 'What will we eat?' or 'What will we drink?' or 'What will we wear?' For it is the Gentiles who strive for all these things; and indeed <u>your heavenly Father knows that you need all these things</u>.

<u>But strive first for the Kingdom of God and his righteousness, and all these things will be given to you as well</u>.

Let us therefore now therefore turn our full attention to the Kingdom of God. For in doing so we will see the amazing connection between the Kingdom that Jesus refers to and the Kingdom that is a key feature of modern Kabbalah.

Chapter 7 –
Kingdom

It is noteworthy if not also a surprise to learn that the phrase 'Kingdom of God' actually only occurs once in the Torah. In contrast, the phrase 'Kingdom of God' or its equivalents, 'Kingdom of Heaven' or 'Kingdom of my Father', occurs over fifty times throughout the gospels of Matthew, Mark, Luke and John.

Although we must be cautious when approaching what Jesus purportedly said, as demonstrated earlier in the book, the 'Kingdom' is repeated constantly throughout the Synoptic Gospels, hence it is both logical and reasonable to infer with high certainty that it was a central theme of Jesus' message.

Very early in the Gospel of Matthew he tells us that;

"Jesus went throughout Galilee, teaching in the synagogues and proclaiming the good news of <u>the Kingdom</u> and curing every disease and every sickness among the people"

[Matthew 4:23]

Likewise, in Luke he says that Jesus tells the crowd before him:

"I must proclaim the good news of the <u>Kingdom</u> of God to the other cities also; for I was sent for this purpose. So he continued proclaiming the message in the synagogues of Judea."

[Luke 4:43]

The rest of Matthew and Luke abound with references to the Kingdom. In fact, this 'good news' is precisely what we are told Jesus instructs his disciples to preach. Jesus does not instruct the disciples to preach anything else.

"Then Jesus called the twelve together and gave them power and authority over all demons and to cure diseases, and he sent them out to proclaim the <u>Kingdom</u> of God and to heal."

[Luke 9:10]

and again;

"Cure the sick who are there, and say to them, 'The <u>Kingdom</u> of God has come near to you"

[Luke 10:9]

But he warns them that once the process of metanoia has begun, once on the spiritual path – it is hard work and there is no going back. The only way is forward.

"No one who puts a hand to the plough and looks back is fit for the <u>Kingdom</u> of God"

[Luke 9:62]

This invites the question 'what is the Kingdom that is being referred to'? What is Jesus referring to? In the Synoptic Gospels this question is repeatedly asked of and answered by Jesus. Is it an actual, secular, temporal, worldly Kingdom? The answer is clearly 'No'.

There cannot be any room for doubt that Jesus is referring to a non - temporal Kingdom. He is alluding to a spiritual Kingdom – what we would now call a state of being - a state of consciousness.

At no stage does Jesus claim to be seeking to establish a Kingdom in the way that, for example Cesar, Genghis Kahn, Alexander the Great, David, or Elizabeth I were, as temporal emperors, rulers, kings and queens.

Jesus was fully aware of the distinction between such types of ruler. His opponents tried to entrap him on the issue and when they did his response was:

"Give to the emperor the things that are the emperor's, and to God the things that are God's"

[Mark 12:17]

In the end we are told in each of the synoptic Gospels that Jesus was taunted and mocked whilst he was on the cross for not being an earthly king – for failing to overthrow in military terms the occupying Romans and the Jewish Religious establishment.

"Those who passed him derided him, shaking their heads and saying ''Aha! You would destroy the temple and build it in three days, save yourself from the cross!''

"In the same way the chief priests, along with the scribes, were also mocking him among themselves and saying. ''He saved others; he cannot save himself. Let the Messiah, the King of Israel, come down from the cross now, so that we may see and believe''.

Those who were crucified with him also taunted him"

[Mark 15:29]

Throughout his ministry Jesus is never reported as attacking the occupying Romans nor their civil jurisdiction. He does not challenge the temporal authorities. Indeed, in one memorable instance he is reported as healing the daughter of a Roman Centurion and applauds the Centurion for his faith.

"When he entered Capernaum, a centurion came to him, appealing to him and saying, "Lord, my servant is lying at home paralyzed, in terrible distress." And he said to him, "I will come and cure him." The centurion answered, "Lord, I am not worthy to have you come under my roof; but only speak the word,

and my servant will be healed. For I also am a man under authority, with soldiers under me; and I say to one, 'Go,' and he goes, and to another, 'Come,' and he comes, and to my slave, 'Do this,' and the slave does it." When Jesus heard him, he was amazed and said to those who followed him, "Truly I tell you, in no one in Israel have I found such faith. I tell you, many will come from east and west and will eat with Abraham and Isaac and Jacob in the Kingdom of heaven, while the heirs of the Kingdom will be thrown into the outer darkness, where there will be weeping and gnashing of teeth." And to the centurion Jesus said, "Go; let it be done for you according to your faith." And the servant was healed in that hour."

[Matthew 8:5-13]

Jesus's message is to shift the focus of our life (metanoia) and in the process we will begin to experience the Kingdom. As we make that shift, the Kingdom will (and this is the Greek word εγγίζω 'enzigo') 'come near', ' be drawn near' or 'be close'. In the sense that the Kingdom belongs to God – it can be said that the Kingdom or presence of God has come – here and now. It is already everywhere, to be found in all things.

Since God is everywhere and in all things (including you and I) – since God is the Source of all things - the Kingdom is at hand - literally and metaphorically. The other sense of come near or drawn near alludes to the future. It is that the Kingdom is making itself felt but it has not fully arrived or materialized. It is yet to materialize. It will materialise once the process of metanoia is completed. As the process of metanoia proceeds, so your aim and target comes into sight and nearer – the shift moves you from one target to another – from one spiritual level to another. From being unconscious to conscious.

This idea of an imminent possibility of God's Kingdom drawing near is found in what is known to Christians as the 'Lord's Prayer'. It is perhaps striking that nowhere else in the New Testament is it claimed that Jesus directly taught a prayer or hymn to his disciples during his public ministry. So, it might be worth looking at it more closely.

This is the Prayer that Jesus is said to have taught his disciples:

'Our Father (Abba) in heaven
Hallowed be your name

Your Kingdom come, Your will be done,
on Earth as it is in Heaven…

[**Matthew 6:10**] - [My emphasis]

There is a great deal of academic learning concerning the original wording of the 'Lord's Prayer'. Almost certainly, the original version was shorter and thus easier to remember. Academic exegesis suggests that the original version is: (John Meier, A Marginal Jew II);

Address	**'Abba' or Father**

'You' Petition   **1. Hallowed be your name**
                              2. Your Kingdom draw near

'We' Petition   **1. Our daily bread give us today**
                            2. And forgive us our debts
                                  As we forgive our debtors
                            3. And do not lead us to the test

The brevity and directness of the prayer points to an immediacy and intimacy with God - in the nature of a father and child relationship. The Aramaic word 'Abba' which means 'Father' has come down to us into the original Greek translation. As we shall see, the word Abba also is an important word in Kabbalah. But when all the academic investigation is done, still at its heart is the clear understanding that Heaven is attainable here on Earth. This is a fundamental aspect of the Lord's Prayer – and of course the core teaching of Jesus.

The linking of the 'Kingdom' and the verb 'engizo' (to come, to draw near) in a prayer-petition is unknown in the Torah, ancient Judaism before Jesus, and in the rest of the New Testament. The idea of a Kingdom would seem to be a deliberate choice and central to the teaching of Jesus.

What Does Jesus Say About The Kingdom?

If the Kingdom, or heaven, is not to be found in the ways of the world, where and when is it to be found? In modern language we use the word 'consciousness' to describe the level to which and at which we have awareness of our egoic selves, of others and awareness of our relationship to God – the Creator, the Light, Allah, the un-sourced source – the One. The higher the level of consciousness is the closer we are in 'Christian' terms to 'Heaven', and in Kabbalah terms – the source of the 'Light'.

The fact that each level of consciousness is achievable as a consequence of the process of metanoia means that Heaven (or the Light) is near at hand to us and can be drawn near or revealed.

It is interesting to note that Jesus does not give a direct answer to the question 'what is the Kingdom of God like?'. It appears to be beyond adequate everyday words. He always says - it is 'like' something. He uses 'parables' that point to different qualities to describe different aspects of the Kingdom. It is no one thing.

To understand 2000 years later what Jesus is teaching, it might help to substitute the words 'Kingdom of God' or 'Heaven' with the word 'Consciousness' or 'Light'.

So, when you read what I say below about 'the Kingdom of God', 'Kingdom of Heaven' or 'Heaven' – replace those words with 'Consciousness' or 'the Light' (or whatever equivalent words you prefer) – and you will get a better understanding and indeed a direct parallel of what Jesus is explaining to his audience of 2000 years ago.

In each instance he is using language and images that will be familiar to his audience. He does not talk down to people but talks in a way that everyone should be able to understand at their respective level of consciousness – the extent to which they are connected to the Light.

In the time of Jesus and even still today, Galilee is a fertile, rural and agricultural area. The audience to who Jesus describes the Kingdom is involved in farming and fishing – and related work. Thus, the content of the parables reflects that context. Those listening to Jesus's stories would have found themselves in a familiar scene where everything is presented with an almost (but deceptively) childlike simplicity. Everywhere behind the Greek text (from which our English translation descends) we get glimpses of Jesus' mother tongue (Aramaic) and the use of circumstances and practices that to us seem strange but were entirely familiar to Jesus' listeners. For example, in the parable of the sower in Mark 4:3-8, the sowing seems so clumsy that much of the seed is wasted. But Jesus was describing the then common practice. In Israel of his time, sowing preceded the ploughing.

In 21st century Kabbalah teaching, the vocabulary used point to modern concepts of new sciences such as psychology, physics and computers. These are the so-called 'New Age' tools and terminology with which we today are familiar. Thus words such as 'ego' 'power', 'energy', 'consciousness', 'dimensions', 'big bang' and so forth – are all relatively new vocabulary and concepts but they conjure up for us images and ideas that would be alien to a 1st century farmer or fisherman in Galilee.

Finally, I invite you to bear in mind that when looking at the parables and my commentaries, remember that what is being described is a spiritual Kingdom - of God. What is being described is beyond our five senses of touch, sight, hearing, smelling and tasting.

Parables – Some further notes of Caution

Before looking in detail at the various parables that answer the question: 'what is the Kingdom like?', I would like to explain why it is necessary to view the parables with a certain degree of caution.

As I pointed out at the beginning of this book, whenever we are looking at what the Synoptic Gospels say about Jesus and the words he said, we should remember that what we are reading is:

- A written record of something that was originally an oral tradition of what Jesus is reported as saying at least 30 years previously.
- The oral tradition would have started in Aramaic and been translated into Greek, then Latin and finally (in our case) English. Inevitably things will have changed as a result of the process of translation.

- What was originally said by Jesus would have undergone some element of editing and process of change, to reflect not necessarily on what Jesus said but what his audience understood him to be saying.

Moreover, in the case of the parables there are additional reasons to suppose that we need to look at what is written with a degree of caution. Here are some pointers:

- Jesus was not reading a script. He was addressing a live audience. His remarks were 'off the cuff'. Jesus was called to provide an on the spot answer to crucial questions.
- Imagine Jesus standing in front of a group of people – a crowd. He would have to be careful in what he said. His audience was a mixed bunch – not everyone receptive to what he was saying. If we are to accept what we read in the synoptic gospels, the audience included not just 'ordinary' folk, but also scribes, Pharisees, other people from the religious establishment and even Roman soldiers.
- The point being here is that what Jesus said (and did) was primarily directed at Jews – not Christians. Christians did not exist when Jesus was talking and explaining what the Kingdom [of God] was like – to what it could be compared to.
- There is evidence from academic studies within the written Synoptic gospels themselves that the parables underwent changes.

- Mainstream academic study (form criticism and related techniques) also shows that the parables were 'altered' so that they were understood and applied to the members of the early church and how the church should conduct itself. Allegorical interpretations were added when originally none were given.
- The early church had to change its position from proclaiming an imminent arrival of the New Age - the Messiah - and to re-interpret the parables to itself in circumstances where the arrival of the Messiah (of the Torah) was delayed.

Above all and making due allowances for the above, it is important to remember that when Jesus is explaining what the Kingdom is like, he is explaining what was the fundamental aspect of his preaching and of his purpose for being – as a messenger. In summary it is:

- A call to personal action i.e. Metanoia – a change of attitude – a change in direction - a shift in focus; and
- The Kingdom is entirely concerned with spirituality - it is a state of being connected to God
- The Kingdom is within reach. It is attainable.

In short, the parables like all the messages of Jesus were concerned with the spiritual relationship with God and the spiritual work needed to be in a state of being connected to God. The parables and all that Jesus is reported as saying should be considered with each of the above factors in mind.

What is a parable?

The Oxford English dictionary defines a parable as;

"A short, simple story designed to illustrate some truth - a simple story to reveal a moral or spiritual lesson"

It is a feature of the Synoptic Gospels that Jesus is almost immediately and frequently reported as speaking in, to people who listened what he had to say. At the same time, these 'parables' also were deployed as a technique for explaining the hidden meaning only to his followers.

According to the highly regarded Catholic Biblical Scholar **John P. Meir** in his book **A Marginal Jew**

'In all the rabbinic literature, not one single 'parable' has come down to us from the period before Jesus.'

'Parables' are unique to Jesus and entirely new.

The fact that the parables contained hidden meanings is reported time and again in the Gospels. Jesus was apparently only willing to reveal the hidden meaning to his twelve disciples and trusted followers.

"When he was alone, those who were around him along with the twelve asked him about the parables. And he said to them, ''To you has been given the secret of the Kingdom of God, but for those outside, everything comes in parables;

[in order that 'they may indeed look, but not perceive, and may listen, but not understand, so that they may not turn again and be forgiven...']

[Mark 4:10]

"With many such parables he spoke the word to them, as they were able to hear it; he did not speak to them except in parables, but he explained everything in private to his disciples"

[Mark 4:33]

Jesus is reported as being asked by his disciples;

"Why do you speak in parables?"

He answered,

''To you [the disciples] it has been given to know the secrets of the Kingdom of heaven''.

[Matthew 13:10-17]

Again in Luke;

"To you it has been given to know the secrets of the Kingdom of God; but to others I speak in parables."

[Luke 8:10]

'You have hidden these things from the wise and the intelligent and have revealed them to infants.'

[Luke 10:21]

However, given the number of times the parables are explained by Jesus to his Disciples, it would seem that the hidden and secret meaning is not even obvious to them. How can this be?

Why Secret? Why a hidden meaning?

For a Rabbi (teacher) whose mission is to teach people

"Metanoia for the Kingdom is at hand"

why would Jesus wish to keep secrets that might preclude people from entering into that highly treasured and valuable Kingdom?

There are various possible answers to this.

Firstly: Jesus knew that the hidden meanings if revealed would be perceived by the Jewish religious leaders as a threat to them. I shall revert to this point shortly. As a

148

result, he knew that his life and that of his followers would be in mortal danger.

Jesus' main message 'Metanoia for the Kingdom is at hand' was a direct challenge to the established religious leaders in these ways:

1. The call to metanoia is a call to take personal responsibility for change – not necessarily requiring the intercedence of the priests or religious observances.
2. The emphasis shifts from a strict observance of the letter of the Law (Torah) – including, sacrifices and other man made rituals - to simply obeying the two most important 'commandments';

   i.   Love God
   ii.   Love your neighbour as yourself

3. This might be explained as a teaching to shift from religious observance to spirituality.

Secondly: The Kingdom is near at hand and can be enjoyed 'on earth as it is in heaven'. To understand that imminence and the 'abundance' that is 'on tap' would be too much to comprehend and accept by everyone. In modern parlance, we would say it would be 'too much to handle'. The Light would be blinding to all except a few.

Thirdly: The parables will only have meaning to anyone that is interested in or concerned with spiritual growth. To anyone else, it is as though Jesus is talking nonsense that has no place in the real world. Isn't this what many people - even religious people say about other religions, Christianity and Kabbalah today?

In other words, to those who accept the Kingdom as being real and are willing to do the work necessary (metanoia) to enter (insiders) - there is no secret.

But those who do not accept the Kingdom and what is needed to enter it – are precluded from knowing and understanding. As a result, they exclude themselves from the Kingdom.

What Jesus is reported as saying is not so much his judgment or decision to withhold as simply a statement of the factual position.

Thus, if you are a seeker of the truth you will understand more and more, both in amount and depth of understanding. But if you are not interested then the opposite is the case. Jesus explains that to outsiders what he says is incomprehensible or of no meaning. To them it is a riddle since even though they see and hear they

"do not perceive…do not listen."

These direct reports of hidden and secret meanings to which 'insiders' alone can understand - certainly point to evidence that Jesus was a Kabbalist. This is especially so when we come to look more closely (as we shall) at what he was saying and doing that so amazed everyone. Of course, once it is appreciated that Jesus (Rabbi Yeshua) is a Kabbalist, these allusions to some hidden source of power and authority make sense. Moreover, the content of what he is reported as saying and doing becomes more profound and significant.

Whilst Jesus makes it clear that his messages are secret and hidden, he repeatedly issues an injunction for his followers and his audience to listen, see and think carefully about what he is saying in the parables.

This gives rise to several points:

1. The 'hidden' meaning in the parables is in principle capable of being understood by everyone.
2. But to understand the eyes have to do more than see – they have to discern by careful observation. The ears have to do more than listen, they have to process what they hear to understand.
3. In short, you have to be focused. You must be willing to perceive and the senses have to be used in conjunction with heart, soul, mind and spirit.

To see at a glance what Jesus is pointing to, the table below forms a non-exhaustive list of the numerous references to the injunction to 'Listen/Hear' and 'See/Perceive'.

	Matthew	Mark	Luke
Listen/hear	7:24 – 26, 13:3-9, 13:10-11, 13:15-19, 13:43	4:9-12, 4:33	8:8, 10:16
See/perceive	13:10, 15:14-20, 16:9-12	4:9-12, 7:18, 8:17, 8:18,	8:9 – 10, 10:21, 10:23, 12:54.

With all of the above in mind, let us now turn to what else Jesus reportedly says about the Kingdom.

Seed & Yeast - Hidden Power

"With what can we compare the Kingdom of God, or what parable will we use for it? It is like a mustard seed, which when sown upon the ground, is the smallest of all the seeds on earth; yet when it is sown it grows up and becomes the greatest of all shrubs, and puts forth large branches, so that the birds of the air can make nests in its shade"

[Mark 4:30]

"What is the Kingdom of God like? And to what should I compare it? It is like a mustard seed that someone took and sowed in the garden; it grew and

152

became a tree, and the birds of the air made nests in its branches''

[Luke 13: 18]

Jesus compares the Kingdom to a seed. The mustard seed is indeed, very small. He explains that despite being small it contains within it a life force and all that is necessary for its growth and expansion literally above and beyond its apparent constraints.

The seed is sown on the earth and without anyone knowing how, it grows in all directions, taking roots, sprouting upwards towards the light and reaching out in all directions. In the process the seed transforms from something very little into something that is far larger and of more value to other sentient beings.

The Kingdom is a hidden life force within us that is at the root of all spiritual growth that reaches to the Light - thus providing an environment that provides a home for all who reside within it. This hidden and mysterious quality is specifically alluded to:

"The Kingdom of God is as if someone would scatter seed on the ground, and would sleep and rise night and day, and the seed would sprout and grow, <u>he does not know how</u>".

[Mark 4:26]

In the same way, the Kingdom can be compared to yeast.

"It is like yeast that a woman took and mixed in with three measures of flour until all of it was leavened."

[Luke 13:21]

Like a mustard seed, yeast comprises of tiny particles that on the face of it bear little resemblance to the ultimate, end product. The transformation is ostensibly miraculous. Without knowing scientifically like we do today the role that yeast plays in producing leavened bread, it would have been common knowledge to Jews that it was yeast that made the bread rise. They realised that yeast contained within it something that was hidden and yet had the power to transform what would otherwise be unleavened (flat) bread into leavened (risen) bread - bread that expanded in all directions and especially upwards. Nowadays, we would say that yeast acts as a catalyst or provides an energy that interacts at a chemical level to produce something far greater than its constituent parts. A polymer. But even today, it is an amazing thing to think that contained within such a small particle there is a potential energy waiting to be unleashed to such great effect.

The Kingdom, Consciousness, the Light likewise also contains that hidden energy potential for transformation. It is a mystery but we have faith (a knowing without knowledge) in its effect.

Children/Greatest/Least/First/Last - Humility

"Let the little children come to me; do not stop them; for it is too such as these that the Kingdom of God belongs. Truly I tell you, whoever does not receive the Kingdom of God as a little child will never enter it"

[Mark 10: 14]

In comparing the Kingdom to a child, Jesus was emphasizing a number of features of being a child. A child is not yet fully 'corrupted' by the ways of the world and is open to be taught the truth. The innocence of a child points to a state of being receptive, that is open, playful, and joyful. Because of the lowly status of children in 1st century Israel, it also points to a state of humility and it is perhaps humility above all that Jesus is directing our attention to. Further, it also points to the fact that it is necessary to first be a child, or possess the aforementioned qualities to have the potential to grow – spiritually. Such qualities are required to be in the Kingdom, but are also affirmative signs of being in it. You will discern it in yourself and others. Jesus is pointing to the process of change to an individual's ego that is required to bring about a reduction in the influence of Satan (the opponent – that little voice in the head) and metanoia, a shift towards and a reception of God's way for the world.

Time and again throughout the Gospels Jesus emphasizes the need for humility in order to gain access to the Kingdom of heaven.

**"Truly I tell you, unless you change and become like
children, you will never enter the Kingdom of heaven.
Whoever becomes humble like this child is the
greatest in the Kingdom of heaven".**

[Matthew 18:4]

The idea of less as more is also a recurring theme.
Humility implies less ego or the total absence of ego. It
is the ego which is the impediment to reaching a higher
level of consciousness of the needs of others.

Wealth/Treasure in Heaven/Treasure in a Field/Fine Pearl

Jesus compares the Kingdom to something of great value
– actually the greatest of value. It is worth sacrificing
everything for it. As in many other instances, Jesus
invites us to turn our assumed values on their heads. This
too is part of the process of metanoia.

His advice is clear, to the rich man who recites the Ten
Commandments to Jesus and assures him that he
observes them. The rich man is invited to shift his
understanding of what is of true worth.

**"Jesus looking at him loved him and said, 'You lack
one thing; go, sell what you own, and give the money
to the poor, and you will have treasure in heaven;
then come, follow me".**

[Mark 10:21]

But it is not an easy task.

"How hard will it be for those who have wealth to enter the Kingdom of God!...It is easier for a camel to go through the eye of a needle than for someone who is rich to enter the Kingdom of God."

But it is not impossible and the outcome is worth the effort.

The value of living in the Kingdom; from being in a state of being that is the Kingdom, where all of our energy and resources should first be applied.

"The Kingdom of Heaven is like treasure hidden in a field which someone found and hid; then in his joy he goes and sells all that he has and buys that field."

[Matthew 13:44]

It is worth giving up everything and it is necessary to be prepared to give up everything to live in the Kingdom. Being prepared to do something is not the same as doing it. The point is, that being prepared is a state of being.

"Again, the Kingdom of heaven is like a merchant in search of fine pearls; on finding one pearl of great value, he went and sold all that he had and bought it."
[Matthew 13:44]

There are many things of value to us as human beings but the Kingdom is the greatest in value and should be treasured. The steps required to be in the Kingdom might even extend to great personal and physical sacrifice. But not necessarily.

"If your hand causes you to stumble, cut it off; it is better for you to enter life maimed than to have two hands and go to hell, to the unquenchable fire. And of your foot causes you to stumble, cut it off' it is better for you to enter life lame than to have two feet and to be throw into hell. And if your eye causes you to stumble, tear it out; it is better for you to enter the Kingdom of God with one eye than to have two eyes and to be thrown into hell."

[Mark 9:43]

What is being emphasized here is not the wrongdoing – the stumbling, but rather the true value of being in the Kingdom. We are being invited to make choices and act upon them. We are being invited to realise that the spiritual world is where we need to be whole – not the physical world.

We often marvel at the dedication and single mindedness that top athletes demonstrate in their desire to succeed. They make great sacrifices for what is ultimately a temporary and fleeting achievement – a win – a piece of metal and perhaps some fame. And then what? Staying at the top brings additional challenges and it is just as difficult, if not more so than getting there in the first place. We are being invited by Jesus to view achieving and maintaining the state of consciousness, with at least as great intensity and commitment.

"Again, the Kingdom of heaven is like a net that was thrown into the sea and caught fish of every kind; when it was full, they drew it ashore, sat down, and put the good into the baskets but threw away the bad...there will be weeping and gnashing of teeth"

It is a matter of spiritual life and death.

Merciful King/Owner/Landlord/Employer – Mercy & Merit

The Kingdom naturally has a King and Jesus describes the relationship between king and his subjects in ways that can be seen and compared with a master-servant relationship on earth. According to Jesus – in the Kingdom, love and forgiveness will be a feature of the experience. But to be in the Kingdom also requires loving and forgiving others and being merciful. He cites the examples of an earthly King who when settling his accounts forgives the failings of his servant and expects the servant to similarly forgive those with who he deals. We are warned of the dire consequences of not forgiving - of the need to be merciful.

"For this reason the Kingdom of heaven may be compared to a king who wished to settle accounts with his slaves. When he began reckoning, one who

159

owed him ten thousand talents was brought to him; and, as he could not pay, his lord ordered him to be sold together with his wife and children and all his possessions, and payment to be made.

So the slave fell to his knees before him saying 'Have patience with me, and I will pay you everything.' Out of pity for him, the lord of the slave released him and forgave him the debt. But that same slave, as he went out, came upon one of his fellow slaves who owed him one hundred denarii, and seizing him by the throat, he said 'Pay what you owe'. Then his fellow slave fell down and pleased with him, 'Have patience with me, and I will pay you.' But he refused; then he went and threw him into prison until he would pay the debt.

When his fellow slaves saw what happened they were greatly distressed, and they went and reported to their lord all that had taken place. Then his lord summoned him. ''You wicked slave! I forgave you all that debt because you pleaded with me. Should you not have mercy on your fellow slave, as I had mercy on you?'' And in anger his lord handed him over to be tortured until he paid his entire debt.
So my heavenly father will also do to everyone of you, if you do not forgive your brother or sister from your heart.''

[Matthew18:23]

The torture described in this passage symbolises a spiritual torture rather than physical. Being apart or disconnected from God is hell on earth.

Effort

Jesus makes it clear that entrance to the Kingdom must be earned and continual effort made to stay in it. He warns of the risk that it will be taken away. It is not just enough to be a Jew.

"the Kingdom of God will be taken away from you and given to a people that produces the fruits of the Kingdom".

[Matthew 21: 43]

The same warning is presented in the parable of the King who gave a wedding banquet for his son. The opportunity to gain access to the Kingdom of God was first offered to the Jews but now it is open to everyone – but not everyone will succeed.

"The Kingdom of heaven may be compared to a king who gave a wedding banquet for his son. He sent his slaves to call those who had been invited to the wedding banquet, but they would not come.

Again, he sent other slaves, saying, 'Tell those who have been invited: Look, I have prepared my diner,

my oxen and my fat calves have been slaughtered, and everything is ready; come to the wedding banquet.' But they made light of it and went away, one to his farm, another to his business while the rest seized his slaves, mistreated them, and killed them. The king was enraged. He sent his troops, destroyed those murderers, and burned their city. Then he said to his slaves, 'The wedding is ready, but those invited were not worthy. Go therefore into the main streets, and invite everyone you find to the wedding banquet.'

The slaves went out into the streets and gathered all whom they found, both good and bad' so the wedding hall was filled with guests. But when the king came into see the guests, he noticed a man there who was not wearing a wedding robe and he said to him, 'Friend, how did you get in here without a wedding robe?' And he was speechless. Then the king said to the attendants, 'Bind him hand and foot, and throw him into the outer darkness, where there will be weeping and gnashing of teeth. For many are called but few are chosen"

[Matthew 22:2]

A similar example is provided in the Gospel of Luke at 14:15 - 24.

Likewise, it is necessary to be vigilant and take steps, making an effort to achieve a state of readiness.

"The Kingdom of heaven will be like this...Keep awake therefore, for you know neither the day nor the hour"

The effort required to connect or be in Heaven may not be the same for every person. Some may have to work harder than others. Whilst each of us must work – some may have to work harder or longer than others to reach the same outcome. Thus:

"For the Kingdom of heaven is like a landowner who went out early in the morning to hire labourers for his vineyard. After agreeing with the labourers for the usual daily wage, he sent them into his vineyard. When he went out about nine o'clock, he saw others standing idle in the marketplace; and he said to them, 'You also go into the vineyard, and I will pay you whatever is right.' So they went. When he went out again about noon and about three o'clock, he did the same. And about five o'clock he went out and found others standing around; and he said to them, 'Why are you standing here idle all day?' They said to him, 'Because no one has hired us.' He said to them, 'You also go into the vineyard.' When evening came, the owner of the vineyard said to his manager, 'Call the labourers and give them their pay, beginning with the last and then going to the first.' When those hired about five o'clock came, each of them received the usual daily wage. Now when the first came, they thought they would receive more; but each of them also received the usual daily wage. And when they

received it, they grumbled against the landowner, saying, 'These last worked only one hour, and you have made them equal to us who have borne the burden of the day and the scorching heat.' But he replied to one of them, 'Friend, I am doing you no wrong; did you not agree with me for the usual daily wage? Take what belongs to you and go; I choose to give to this last the same as I give to you. Am I not allowed to do what I choose with what belongs to me? Or are you envious because I am generous?' So the last will be first, and the first will be last."

[Matthew 20:1]

What is clear here is that effort is required in order to achieve spiritual growth. We are all given at least some level of spiritual awareness and it is our duty to work with whatever level of awareness we have to achieve more. It is not enough to do nothing. And with growth is the gift of greater insight and reward.

"For it is as if a man, going on a journey, summoned his slaves and entrusted his property to them; to one he gave five talents, to another two, to another one, to each according to his ability. Then he went away. The one who had received the five talents went off at once and traded with them, and made five more talents. In the same way, the one who had the two talents made two more talents. But the one who had received the one talent went off and dug a hole in the ground and hid his maser's money.

After a long time, the master of those slaves came and settled accounts with them.

The one who had received the five talents came forward, bringing five more talents, saying Master, you handed over to me five talents; see, I have made five more talents'.

His master said to him, well done, good and trustworthy slave, you have been trustworthy in a few things, I will put you in charge of many things; enter into the joy of your master.

And the one with the two talents also came forward, saying Master, you handed over to me five talents; see, I have made two more talents'.

His master said to him, well done, good and trustworthy slave, you have been trustworthy in a few things, I will put you in charge of many things; enter into the joy of your master.

Then the one who had received the one talent also came forward, saying, Master, I knew you were a harsh man, reaping where you did not sow, and gathering where you did not scatter seed; so I was afraid, and I went and hid your talent in the ground. Here you have what is yours. But his master replied; You wicked and lazy slave! You knew did you, that I reap where I did not so, and gather where I did not scatter? Then you ought to have invested my money with the bankers, and on my return I would have received what was my own with interest. So take the talent from him, and give it to the one with the ten talents. For to those who have, more will be given, but from those who have nothing, even what they have will be taken away. As for the worthless slave, throw him into the outer darkness, where there will be weeping and gnashing of teeth"

[Matthew 25:14-30]

As with the previous passage – the pain is spiritual.

In summary therefore, Jesus teaches that the Kingdom, the Light:

1. Is within the spiritual realm; and
2. Contains hidden and miraculous powers of transformation and abundance; and
3. Is of ultimate value; and
4. Is open to all; and
5. Is already present and available - is within reach; and
6. Requires personal effort and constant attention; and
7. Requires love, humility, mercy and compassion - in short to treat people as you would like to be treated, 'love thy neighbour as thyself'

It is definitely worth the effort since it is the ultimate treasure, for it brings us into the presence and dominion of God's Light; enlightenment and happiness.
Equally, a failure to make the effort to pursue spiritual growth will result in being excluded from being connected to God, which brings darkness, mental torment, pain and suffering.

Chapter 8 –
Faith, Miracles & Resurrection

The admiration and awe that Jesus draws from those who come into contact with him is not just based on his words but also his actions. The Synoptic Gospels is littered with references to events where Jesus appears to be the agent for what was described at the time as a wondrous deed and what nowadays would be described or referred to as miracles.

According to the Oxford English Dictionary, a miracle is;

"An extraordinary and welcome event that is not explicable by natural or scientific laws and is therefore attributed to a divine agency"

Just as we cannot know with absolute certainty what Jesus said, we cannot know precisely what Jesus did. Some Christians, known as Fundamentalists, believe that the miracles as described in the Synoptic Gospels were actual historical events. Some do not, preferring to see the 'events' as allegorical. We cannot know them to be actual historical events.

The caveats that I mentioned in previous chapters about the limitations of the Synoptic Gospels as historically accurate applies to both what Jesus is reported as saying and what he is reported as doing.

I should say at once that I do believe that miracles can and do happen. As I shall explain in the final chapter, life or existence itself is a miracle – perhaps the ultimate miracle, but I have seen and experienced many minor miracles – things beyond rational explanation.

When we come to look at the miracles connected with Jesus, it seems to me that the existence or occurrence of miracles is not the only impressive aspect of what is described. No, an equally impressive aspect is that he appears to be able to perform miracles or be an agent for them to occur – at will. Many people might say – 'such and such was a miracle'. But few if any people are able to say that they know of someone or have seen someone that can perform miracles at will.

But if we are to believe at face value what we read in the Synoptic Gospels or even something approximating it, then Jesus was able to do that.

In the end, we are left with a choice. Do we believe or do we not believe? Do we believe that the various events recorded in the Synoptic Gospels that might otherwise be described as miracles, actually took place as described – or is there some other rational explanation for what is described? Was someone physically blind and then had their vision physically restored – either directly or indirectly by Jesus? Or is what is described simply a metaphor?

We are then left with a further issue. What is the relevance of a belief (or not) in miracles to the core message of Jesus as previously identified in this book?

"Metanoia, the Kingdom has drawn near."

Or put another way:

"Change the focus of your life from the material to the spiritual and you will enjoy deep and lasting happiness – now"

If I believe that the miracles are actual historical events, does that change what Jesus taught? Conversely, if I do not believe that they were actual historical events, does that change what Jesus taught. In both instances I think that the answer is 'no'. The core message does not change.

As I shall explain, Jesus' message is an essential truth if not the essential truth of not just the message of Jesus, but also Kabbalah and all monotheistic religions.

What however might change is my perception of the validity or authority of the person teaching the message. If that messenger really can perform miracles 'on demand' then there is something rather special about them.

Such a person is clearly connected to a source of energy that is very powerful and that source is beyond everyday levels of experience and consciousness. Perhaps his message points to that source. In short, that person has authority and my attention.

But whilst the core message might not change, the performance of miracles might actually be an endorsement of the message rather than the messenger. In this instance, the validity or authority is not so much in who delivers the message – but in the message itself. It is the message that is enhanced.

'Metanoia, for the Kingdom of God has drawn near.

becomes

'Redirect your Life and you will enjoy deep and lasting happiness - now'

+

Here is a miracle to prove it.

In other words; make a change to your focus and you will be spiritually connected to God. Once connected you can cause miracles to happen. You can affect the temporal world.

In the Sermon on the Mount Jesus says in clear terms:

"Do not worry about your life, what you will eat or what you will drink, or about your body, what you will wear. Is not life more than food, and the body more than clothing?...

But strive first for the Kingdom of God and all his righteousness, and all these things will be given to you as well."

[Matthew 6:25]

This 'striving' is the very metanoia that I have been alluding to. It is the very essence of the message of Jesus. Spirit first – temporal things will take care of themselves.

The miracles seem to fall into four main categories:

- Exorcisms (Unclean spirits)
- Cures for physical ailments (sight, hearing, talking, loss of grip, lameness)
- Control over natural phenomena
- Resurrection of the dead

There are numerous miracle stories in the Synoptic Gospels. But I shall now highlight some interesting features with the use of selected examples.

To illustrate the points that I am going to share with you (see next page), I am simply going to use what is recorded in the Gospel of Mark. But please be assured, what I say here is echoed in each of the two other synoptic Gospels.

Whether you believe that the miracles historically occurred or not, there are some interesting features concerning them that I wish to share with you. It is a matter for you to decide whether and if so to what extent, your belief is in anyway enhanced, confirmed or altered.

Miracles

	Matthew	Mark	Luke
Exorcisms Demons/Unclean spirits	8:28-33, 17:14-19	1:23-26, 3:10-12, 5:2-20	4:33-37, 8:2, 8:27-36, 9:38-43, 11:14
Cures Sight, hearing, speech, limbs	8:1-4, 8:5-13, 8:14-17, 9:2-8, 9:18-21 9:27-30, 9:32-34, 12:10-13, 12:22, 20:30-34	1:30, 1:40, 2:3, 3:2-6, 5:25-34, 6:56, 7:32-37, 8:22-26, 9:21-29, 10:47-52	4:39, 5:12-14, 5:18-20, 6:6, 6:18, 7:2-10, 7:21, 8:43-48, 9:11-17, 13:10-13, 17:12-15
Control – Natural world	14:15-21	4:35-41, 6:37-44 6:48-52, 8:1-9, 9:2-13	5:6-9, 8:22-25, 9:12-17, 9:28-36
Resurrection	9:18- 26	5:35-43	7:12-17, 8:41-55

Unclean Spirits

The Greek term πνεύμα ακάθαρτον 'pneuma akatharton' depending on the precise context and meaning unclean/evil/ demonic spirit or soul, appears twenty (20) times in the New Testament in the context of someone who appears to be possessed.

The role played by the demon or unclean spirit is to cause disease, disability, mental illness and anti-social behaviour. The spirit defiles and causes the individual to suffer physically and spiritually. Exorcism and healing are different but are often closely associated.

The first recorded act of Jesus in his public ministry **[Mark 1:23]** is an exorcism, a not uncommon Jewish magical practice. It is immediately followed by another act of healing **[Mark 1:29-34]** and reference to many similar acts of healing.

Jewish exorcisms were usually preceded by fumigation with incense/smoke and a command for the spirit to leave the individual by means of a charm spoken or on an amulet. The process was expected to last for hours if not days. But when Jesus heals or exorcises (or indeed performs a miracle), there is little or if any preparation and it seems to occur immediately and at will.

"Just then there was a man in their synagogue a man with an unclean spirit, and he cried out 'What have you to do with us?...But Jesus rebuked him saying

'Be silent, and come out of him'. And the unclean
spirit, convulsing him and crying with a loud voice,
came out of him"

There appears to have been no preparation or
incantation. No delay. Jesus simply says 'Be silent and
come out of him' – and he/it does. The impact of those
who witnessed the exorcism is profound:

'They were all amazed...What is this? A new
teaching – with authority!'

[Mark 1:27]

Notice it is the teaching - not Jesus - that is attributed
with the authority – just as it had earlier in the visit to the
synagogue a few lines before this passage.

"They were astounded by his teaching for he taught
as one having authority and not as the scribes."

[Mark 1:22]

Faith/Belief/Prayer

On virtually every occasion Jesus attributes his healing
powers and power over nature to faith or belief. Indeed,
it is probably true to say that the exorcisms and healing
miracles are directly related to faith. They occur only as
a result of faith.

Thus:

"When Jesus saw their faith, he said to the paralytic, 'Son your sins are forgiven'."

[Mark 2:5]

'He woke up and rebuked the wind, and said to the sea, "Peace, be still!" Then the wind ceased, and there was dead calm. He said to them, why are you afraid? Have you still no faith?"

[Mark 4:39]

After the woman who was bleeding was cured simply by touching his cloak:

"Daughter, your faith has made you well; go in peace, and be healed of your disease"

[Mark 5:34]

Conversely, a lack of faith or certainty produces a diminished opportunity for God's power to be revealed. Thus, after the cynicism of those who knew him and Jesus declaring that 'Prophets are not without honour except in their hometown':

"And he could do no deed of power there, except he laid his hands on a few sick people and cured them. And he was amazed at their unbelief."
[Mark 6:5]

After apparently feeding the five thousand people with five fish and two loaves, Jesus sends the disciples in a boat across the sea to Bethsaida. He is seen by his disciples who are;

"straining at the oars against an adverse wind, he came towards them early in the morning walking on the sea. He intended to pass them by...
They were all terrified. But immediately he spoke to them and said, ''Take heart, it is I; do not be afraid. Then he got into the boat with them and the wind ceased.
And they were utterly astounded for they did not understand about the loaves, but their hearts were hardened."
[Mark 6:48-52]

Notice the reference to a lack of understanding about 'the loaves'. This could be alluding to a number of things. But it is not made clear to what he is referring. Being the disciples of Jesus, it begs the question, 'How could they not understand?'

As I explain in more detail below, it seems to me that this is pointing to a metaphorical interpretation that they do not understand rather than a physical event. Notice also and particularly in the present context - the reference to 'hardened hearts'. Someone whose heart is not open to or who does not trust in God – in short means that they are lacking belief or faith.

176

When the disciples could not exorcise the demons in a child:

'You faithless generation, how much longer must I be among you?'

The child's father asks Jesus to help saying;

'If you are able to do anything, have pity on us and help us'.

To which Jesus responds with exasperation:

''If you are able! – All things can be done for the one who believes.''

[Mark 9:19 - 23]

Again after curing a blind beggar:

"Go your faith has made you well. Immediately he regained his sight and followed him on the way"
[Mark 10: 52]

Faith and belief then is the cornerstone of the relationship with God and the power that flows through an individual.
A belief that simply being touched by Jesus would provide a cure.

"They came to Bethsaida. Some people brought a blind man to him and begged him to touch him. He took the blind man by the hand and led him out of the village; and when he had put saliva on his eyes and laid his hands on him, he asked him, "Can you see anything?" And the man looked up and said, "I can see people, but they look like trees, walking." Then Jesus laid his hands on his eyes again; and he looked intently and his sight was restored, and he saw everything clearly. Then he sent him away to his home, saying, "Do not even go into the village."

[Mark 8:22-26]

It is faith and belief that form the substratum of the healing and exorcisms. It is repeated time and again and as though to emphasise the point Jesus says:

"Have faith in God. Truly I tell you, if you say to this mountain, "Be taken up and thrown into the sea", and if you do not doubt it in your heart, but believe that what you say will pass, it will be done for you."

[Mark 11:22-23]

What then is such a faith? How can it be achieved? We are told in the very next line. Jesus says something that is echoed in Kabbalah and has been picked up by many of today's leading New Age spiritual teachers. It is often overlooked and under emphasized in the Christian traditions:

'Whatever you ask for in prayer, believe that you have received it, and it will be yours'. (Mark 11:24)

The profoundness and the power of this short simple statement cannot be over stated. Prayer is not about begging or beseeching. The Hebrew word for prayer is תפלה *Tefillah*. It is a form of service to fulfil the Biblical command: "'You shall serve God with your whole heart.''

Here is the teaching as I understand it:

- Prayer is a state of being connected to God
- That state of being is as a heart to heart.
- In that state of being – you are connected to and in the Light
- In a state of Prayer, you 'know' that whatever you ask for will be given.

Please note that Jesus is not reported here as saying pray (the verb) for something. He is saying **in** [a state of] prayer asking (the verb).

'Whatever you ask for <u>in</u> prayer, believe that you have received it, and it will be yours'.

Being in a state of prayer (as described above) will influence what you ask for and the degree of your faith in receiving it. Faith here is a state of knowing and certainty.

Jesus is Not the Healer – it is Faith in God

Jesus makes it clear that he does not wish to claim credit for the miracle. He strives instead to distance himself from the benefit that is bestowed upon the individual that is cured, healed or exorcised.

Jesus is repeatedly reported as instructing the individual not to tell anyone about what had happened. The individual is instructed to not tell anyone and instead to simply go about their business and/or give thanks in the synagogue.

'And he cured many who were sick with various diseases, and cast out many demons; and he would not permit the demons to speak, because they knew him.'
[Mark 1: 34]

After curing a leper:

'See that you say nothing to anyone; but go, show yourself to the priest, and offer your cleansing what Moses commanded as a testimony to them'.
[Mark 1: 44]

After exorcising the man with a legion of evil spirits – the thanks are to be given to God not Jesus:
'Go home to your friends, and tell them how much the Lord has done for you and what mercy he has shown you.'

[Mark 5:19]

After restoring the sight of a blind man:

'Then he sent him away to his home, saying, ''Do not even go into the village.''
[Mark 8:26]

Controlling Natural Phenomena – Mind over Matter

On the face of it, the ability to control or alter natural phenomena such as the wind and other physical objects is difficult to explain. Either they happened or they are metaphors showing the extent to which faith or certainty can bring about spiritual transformation.

The first recorded event is when Jesus stops a storm, the wind from blowing and creates a state of calm. Here is what is described:

"On that day, when evening had come, he said to them, "Let us go across to the other side." And leaving the crowd behind, they took him with them in the boat, just as he was. Other boats were with him. A great windstorm arose, and the waves beat into the boat, so that the boat was already being swamped. But he was in the stern, asleep on the cushion; and they woke him up and said to him, "Teacher, do you not care that we are perishing?" He woke up and rebuked the wind, and said to the sea,

"Peace! Be still!" Then the wind ceased, and there was a dead calm. He said to them, "Why are you afraid? Have you still no faith?" And they were filled with great awe and said to one another, "Who then is this, that even the wind and the sea obey him?"

[Mark 4:35]

"Immediately he made his disciples get into the boat and go on ahead to the other side, to Bethsaida, while he dismissed the crowd. After saying farewell to them, he went up on the mountain to pray.
When evening came, the boat was out on the sea, and he was alone on the land. When he saw that they were straining at the oars against an adverse wind, he came towards them early in the morning, walking on the sea. He intended to pass them by. But when they saw him walking on the sea, they thought it was a ghost and cried out; for they all saw him and were terrified. But immediately he spoke to them and said, "Take heart, it is I; do not be afraid." Then he got into the boat with them and the wind ceased. And they were utterly astounded, for they did not understand about the loaves, but their hearts were hardened."

[Mark 6: 45 – 52]

Both passages are full of Kabbalah symbolism, references and metaphors. Faith in matters of spirituality is the key.

- Sea or water is Life here on Earth
- Wind is spiritual energy – it is God's energy
- The boat is a vessel – just as each of us humans are vessels.
- The vessels are prone to being knocked around and swamped by the events of Life.
- Land here symbolizes stability and security. God.

By walking on the sea, Jesus is demonstrating his mastery of life both spiritual and temporal. He had been alone on land – that is having his feet and person stable and secure. He could walk on (or through) life – i.e. water, because he was starting from a secure source – land - God.

Just as for many Christians and Kabbalists too, it is entirely possible that the events depicted were actual physical historical events. We cannot know of course but in any event, the Kabbalah message is clear.

Jesus is in control of life. Faith, trust and surrendering to God will enable us to be in control of life. There is nothing to fear.

There are then two versions of the feeding of a large crowd of people with what otherwise would be understood to be a totally inadequate amount of food.

"Taking the five loaves and the two fish, he looked up to heaven, and blessed and broke the loaves, and gave them to his disciples to set before the people; and he divided the two fish among them all. And all ate and

were filled; and they took up twelve baskets full of broken pieces and of the fish. Those who had eaten the loaves numbered five thousand men."

[Mark 6:41-44]

Again, to Kabbalists what is described in this miracle may have actually taken place. But certainly the passage is loaded with Kabbalistic metaphors.

In Kabbalah fish are a sign of mercy. There are two fish and this may be a reference to the male and female duality of creation. Mercy is granted to both men and women.

Often bread is a reference to the ego. People like bread are swelled up with their own importance. But here, it is likely that the bread is meant to be spiritual sustenance. What Jesus has to say is feeding or nourishing everyone spiritually – compared to the yeast of the Pharisees.

There are five books in the Torah. The Torah is what sustains and provides strength. The twelve baskets are reference to the twelve tribes of Israel being filled – or rather being fulfilled. Twelve represents totality, wholeness, and the completion of God's purpose. There are twelve (12) months in the year, and twelve (12) houses of the zodiac.

"He asked them, "How many loaves do you have?" They said, "Seven." Then he ordered the crowd to sit

down on the ground; and he took the seven loaves, and after giving thanks he broke them and gave them to his disciples to distribute; and they distributed them to the crowd. They had also a few small fish; and after blessing them, he ordered that these too should be distributed. They ate and were filled; and they took up the broken pieces left over, seven baskets full."
[Mark 8:5-8]

The events described in this passage may have actually occurred too.

Nevertheless, the number 'seven' is what this passage is about. Seven is a highly symbolic number in both Judaism and Kabbalah. It is the symbol of Creation. The first verse of the Torah consists of seven Hebrew words.

בראשית ברא אלוהים את השמים ואת הארץ

The process of the completion of Creation is in seven days. In the Zohar, the seven lower *sephirot* are those aspects of God that are present in *asiyah*, our world of action.

Finally, Jesus seems to take a step that seems at odds with all that has gone before. He curses a fig tree. A fig tree has special symbolic significance in Kabbalah as I shall also explain in Chapter 9.

"On the following day, when they came from Bethany, he was hungry. Seeing in the distance a fig

185

tree in leaf, he went to see whether perhaps he would find anything on it. When he came to it, he found nothing but leaves, for it was not the season for figs. He said to it, "May no one ever eat fruit from you again." And his disciples heard it.

[Mark 11:12 -14]

"In the morning as they passed by, they saw the fig tree withered away to its roots"

[Mark 11:20]

"From the fig tree learn its lesson: as soon as its branch becomes tender and puts forth its leaves, you know that summer is near."

[Mark 11:28]

Fig trees normally bear fruit twice a year, in June and in September. A unique aspect of the plant is that it bears fruit before its leaves appear after winter. In the Torah and Kabbalah, the fig tree is a metaphor for Israel as a nation. It often symbolized the health of the nation both spiritually and physically. What Jesus is doing here is prophesizing the judgment that will be inflicted on Israel if it does not bear fruit – spiritual fruit. The unproductiveness of the fig tree symbolized Israel's spiritual barrenness, despite their fervent outward dedication and compliance to the strict letter of the law.

Transfiguration

In each of the Synoptic Gospels an event is reported that seems to be a further instance of Jesus being involved in an event beyond rational explanation. It is known in the Christian religions as the 'Transfiguration of Jesus'. It is the only miracle that happens to Jesus.

The transfiguration passage is in the context of a number of verses immediately prior to it that are specifically directed towards the idea that Jesus is the Messiah.

"Jesus went on with his disciples to the villages of Caesarea Philippi; and on the way he asked his disciples, "Who do people say that I am?" And they answered him, "John the Baptist; and others, Elijah; and still others, one of the prophets." He asked them, "But who do you say that I am?" Peter answered him, "You are the Messiah." And he sternly ordered them not to tell anyone about him.
Jesus Foretells His Death and Resurrection
Then he began to teach them that the Son of Man must undergo great suffering, and be rejected by the elders, the chief priests, and the scribes, and be killed, and after three days rise again. He said all this quite openly. And Peter took him aside and began to rebuke him. But turning and looking at his disciples, he rebuked Peter and said, "Get behind me, Satan! For you are setting your mind not on divine things but on human things."
He called the crowd with his disciples, and said to them, "If any want to become my followers, let them

deny themselves and take up their cross and follow me. For those who want to save their life will lose it, and those who lose their life for my sake, and for the sake of the gospel, will save it. For what will it profit them to gain the whole world and forfeit their life? Indeed, what can they give in return for their life? Those who are ashamed of me and of my words in this adulterous and sinful generation, of them the Son of Man will also be ashamed when he comes in the glory of his Father with the holy angels."

[Mark 8:27-38]

This is what then happens:

Six days later, Jesus took with him Peter and James and John, and led them up a high mountain apart, by themselves. And he was transfigured before them, and his clothes became dazzling white, such as no one on earth could bleach them. And there appeared to them Elijah with Moses, who were talking with Jesus. Then Peter said to Jesus, "Rabbi, it is good for us to be here; let us make three dwellings, one for you, one for Moses, and one for Elijah." He did not know what to say, for they were terrified. Then a cloud overshadowed them, and from the cloud there came a voice, "This is my Son, the Beloved; listen to him!" Suddenly when they looked around, they saw no one with them anymore, but only Jesus.

[Mark 9: 2 – 8]

Again, this event may have been an actual historical event or a later Christian addition that is intended to symbolise the Messianic credentials of Jesus. But there may be another explanation.

The passage is loaded with symbols and images that are found in Kabbalah and I shall refer to those in more detail in Chapter 9.

Resurrection or Restoring Life? Physical or Spiritual?

Apart from the resurrection of Jesus himself, there is only one recorded incidence in the Gospel of Mark of a person being brought 'back to life'. The engagement with natural phenomena is difficult for us to explain away in terms of an historical event.

It is difficult to believe that Jesus physically walked on the sea and that he was able to satisfy the physical appetites of several thousand people with a few loaves and fish – and still leave baskets of food left over.

But when it comes to resurrecting people from being dead? Are we actually witnessing the resurrection of someone who has physically died?
In contrast to the walking on the sea, I think we can all believe that it is at least possible that people saw what they thought was a dead person interacting with Jesus and springing back into life. But is this what is actually

being described? Let us look at what is described more carefully.

The first and only instance of what seems to be a resurrection or an event that brought someone back to life is in Mark, involving the daughter of one of leaders of the synagogue.

"My little daughter is <u>at the point of death</u>. Come and lay your hands on her, so that she may be made well and live"

When he arrives Jesus is temporarily distracted by the woman who had suffered from haemorrhaging for years and who wanted to touch his cloak. You may recall that she was cured by her faith.

"While he was still speaking, some people came from the leader's house to say, ''Your daughter is dead' Why trouble the teacher any further?'' But over hearing what they said, Jesus said to the leader of the synagogue, <u>''Do not fear, only believe'</u>.
He allowed no one to follow him except Peter, James and John the brother of James...people weeping and wailing loudly. He said to them, ''Why do you make a commotion and weep? The child is not dead but sleeping''. And they laughed at him. Then he put them all outside, and took the child's father and mother and those who were with him and went to where the child was. He took her by the hand and said to her, ''Talitha cum'' (טליתה קומי), which means in Aramaic, ''Little girl, get up!'' And immediately she got up and began to walk about (she was twelve

years of age). At this they were overcome with amazement. He strictly ordered them that no one should know this, and told them to give her something to eat"

[Mark 5: 22-43]

It is of course immediately noticeable that:

- The girl's father tells Jesus that the girl is at the point of death.
- Thus - the girl had not yet died when he asked for help.
- It is other people who say that the girl has died.
- Jesus does not say that the girl was dead.
- Jesus does not claim that he has restored her to life.
- Unlike other 'miracles' Jesus does not say that the faith of the child, or her parents has 'cured her' or 'healed her' or 'brought her back to life' – but it may be implied from his initial entreaty to 'only believe'.

It is interesting to contrast what happens here with what happens in the unclean spirits and healing events earlier mentioned. We are not told that the girl is dead and that she is restored to life. We are told that she is sleeping and that Jesus lifts her up.

In mentioning the girls age as being twelve, it might also be reasonable to assume that this is a reference to the girl reaching puberty and adulthood. She is on the brink of maturity physically – and also spiritually. She is being lifted by Jesus from childhood (sleep) to a spiritually higher level – awakened. She has transitioned to adulthood. In the process, she is put on her feet and is able to walk through life.

There are two other occasions where there appears to be a resurrection event. One is mentioned in Luke.

"A man who had died was being carried out. He was his mother's only son, and she was a widow...he had compassion for her and said to her, ''Do not weep''. Then he came forward and touched the bier, and the bearers stood still. And he said, ''Young man, I say to you rise!'' The dead man sat up and began to speak, and Jesus gave him to his mother.
Fear seized all of them; and they glorified God saying, ''A great prophet has risen among us!...''

[Luke 7:11]

Again, as previously mentioned, Luke is one of the two Synoptic Gospels that uses Mark as its main source of material. There is no mention of a resurrection scene in Matthew and the one recounted by Luke bears broad similarities with the one described in Mark. The other resurrection event is the well-known raising of Lazarous which can be found in John 11:1-44. I have previously mentioned that the Gospel of John must be approached with great caution.

This caution is entirely appropriate when looking at the events described by John as they relate to Lazarous. For our purposes, a detailed analysis of John 11: 1-44 does not alter the points being made in this book.

But of course, there is one other instance of someone apparently being 'raised from the dead'. That involved Jesus himself; and it is at the heart of Christian theology.

To be a Christian according to the Christian Creed involves a declaration of belief that Jesus died and was 'resurrected'. But is that the same as Jesus dying and being brought back to life? What did Jesus say about resurrection? In the Gospel of Mark there is a detailed discussion between Jesus and;

"Some Sadducees, who say there is no resurrection, came to him and asked him a question, saying, "Teacher, Moses wrote for us that if a man's brother dies, leaving a wife but no child, the man shall marry the widow and raise up children for his brother. There were seven brothers; the first married and, when he died, left no children; and the second married the widow and died, leaving no children; and the third likewise; none of the seven left children. Last of all the woman herself died. In the resurrection whose wife will she be? For the seven had married her."
Jesus said to them, "<u>Is not this the reason you are wrong, that you know neither the scriptures nor the power of God? For when they rise from the dead</u>, they neither marry nor are given in marriage, but <u>are</u>

like angels in heaven. And as for the dead being raised, have you not read in the book of Moses, in the story about the bush, how God said to him, 'I am the God of Abraham, the God of Isaac, and the God of Jacob'? He is God not of the dead, but of the living; you are quite wrong."

[Mark 12: 18 – 27]

If what Mark records Jesus saying is accurate and true, resurrection is not a physical event. According to Jesus – it is a spiritual event. It is an elevation of consciousness to a higher level. Kabbalah's view of resurrection mirrors this spiritual understanding. With this in mind, let us turn to the resurrection of Jesus as described in the Gospel of Mark. According to Mark, here are the final moments of the life of Jesus:

"Then Jesus gave a loud cry and breathed his last. And the curtain of the temple was torn in two, from top to bottom. Now when the centurion, who stood facing him, saw that in this way he breathed his last, he said, "Truly this man was God's Son!"

[Mark 15: 37 – 39]

According to this account Jesus was quite clearly dead. Let us then look at what is described following Jesus's death - again in Mark - the earliest of the Synoptic Gospels.

"When the Sabbath was over, Mary Magdalene,

Mary the mother of James, and Salome bought spices so that they might go and anoint him. And very early on the first day of the week, when the sun had risen, they went to the tomb. They had been saying to one another, "Who will roll away the stone for us from the entrance to the tomb?"
When they looked up, they saw that the stone, which was very large, had already been rolled back. As they entered the tomb, they saw a young man dressed in a white robe sitting on the right side, and they were alarmed.
But he said to them "Do not be alarmed, "You are looking for Jesus, who was crucified. He has been raised; he is not here. Look there is the place they laid him. But go, tell his disciples and Peter that he is going ahead of you to Galilee; there you will see him, just as he told you.'"
So they went out and fled from the tomb, for terror and amazement had seized them. And they said nothing to anyone, for they were afraid.

[Mark 16: 1 – 8]

Before looking more closely at what is being reported in this passage first let us remind ourselves of the following:

1. As I noted above, Jesus explains that resurrection is a spiritual process – not a physical one. For convenience I repeat the passage again.

    when they rise from the dead, they... are like

195

angels in heaven. And as for the dead being raised, have you not read in the book of Moses, in the story about the bush, how God said to him, 'I am the God of Abraham, the God of Isaac, and the God of Jacob'? He is God not of the dead, but of the living; you are quite wrong."

[Mark 12: 24 – 27]

2. In the context of the views expressed by Jesus this is what Mark records Jesus saying about what will happen after he is crucified:

'But after I am **raised up**, I will go before you to Galilee'

[Mark 14:28]

Notice how the same word **'raised'** [or **'rise'**] is being utilised in both contexts.

In the light of the above we can now look at the passage when the three women go the burial chamber and note the following.

- Jesus is referred to as Jesus – not Jesus the Messiah or Jesus the Saviour.
- Mary the mother of Jesus is not mentioned.
- Why would the young man in a white robe state the obvious? - **"You are looking for Jesus, who was crucified"**

- Jesus was crucified. He does not actually say that Jesus is dead – though it may be reasonable to infer it, not least by what he says next.
- The person in white says of Jesus - '**He has been raised**'. Pausing for reflection there.
    - (1) We have just seen that Jesus talks about being 'raised' and going to Galilee - and
    - (2) In the context of a discussion with Sadducees (who did not believe in resurrection) Jesus clarifies what being 'raised' means - '**they rise from the dead, they… are like angels in heaven**'. So, Jesus having been '**raised**' is like an angel in heaven – a spiritual entity.
- But note also that the young man in a white robe declares of Jesus - '**He is not here. Look there is the place they laid him**'.
- Of course, this does not explicitly state that the dead body of Jesus is not still laid out in the tomb. It is entirely consistent with what Jesus told the Sadducees that Jesus' dead body was still in the tomb but the spirit has been raised to heaven as an angel – and therefore 'not here'. *[When my grandmother Esther died, it was of the most enormous comfort to me when the priest pointing at her coffin declared that whilst Esther's body is in the coffin in front of us, her soul had gone to heaven. She was not 'here'.]*
- The person in white then says of Jesus: '**he is going ahead of you to Galilee; there you will see him, just as he told you**'. Actually, as I have

just shown, according to Mark that is not what Jesus told them. Jesus did not say he would be seen in Galilee. What he actually said was: **'But after I am raised up, I will go before you to Galilee.'**

- The three women do not tell anyone about what they had seen and heard.
- There is no reference to any of the disciples seeing Jesus in any form either at the tomb or in Galilee or anywhere.

It gets more intriguing.

You will recall that I mentioned at Chapter 3. that there were different versions of the Bible and that it is an evolving work. In fact, there are at least two alternative endings to the Gospel of Mark.

A shorter ending and a longer ending.

These different endings are mentioned in the New Revised Standard Version of the New Testament.
In the footnote to the ending of Mark at 16: 8 here is what it says:

Footnote 7
'Some of the most ancient authorities bring the Gospel of Mark to a close at the end of verse 8'.

In the Gospel of Mark, the ending is:

'So they went out and fled from the tomb, for terror and amazement had seized them; and they said nothing to anyone, for they were afraid.'

[Mark 16:8]

END OF GOSPEL. The Gospel of Mark in the ancient authorities ends at this point.

But the Editors of the New Revised Standard Version then explain in footnote 8 that there are two alternative endings – one of which is known as the Shorter ending and the other the Longer ending.

"One authority concludes the book with the shorter ending; others conclude the shorter ending and then continue with verses 9-20. In most authorities, verses 9-20 follow immediately after verse 8, though in some of these authorities the passage is marked as doubtful"

This is rather important since the Christian faith turns on the authenticity and certainty (not doubt) of these endings of 'doubtful' authority. In the absence of what is reported in the Shorter and/or Longer endings there is no evidence in the Gospel of Mark – the closest in time to the death of Jesus of the Gospels to be written – that Jesus was seen after his death. The resurrection if it took place would then be entirely in keeping with what Jesus is reported as saying resurrection was like – becoming an angel – being raised to a higher spiritual level.

See Mark 12:24-27 above.

Let us now look at these two controversial and 'doubtful' endings.

The Shorter Ending of Mark

'And all that had been commanded them they told briefly to those around Peter. And afterward Jesus himself sent out through them, from east to west, the sacred and imperishable proclamation of eternal salvation.'

Again – there are some interesting things to note here:

- 'Them' presumably refers to **Mary Magdalene, Mary the mother of James, and Salome.** But it does not expressly say so.
- All that had been commanded then presumably refers to **'But go, tell his disciples and Peter that he is going ahead of you to Galilee; there you will see him, just as he told you'.**
- We have noted that Jesus did not tell them this.
- Moreover, instead of telling the disciples and Peter as purportedly commanded - according to what is described after the women met the young man in a white robe they fled the scene and - **They said nothing to anyone, for they were afraid.**
- Also – why would the instruction be to tell **those around** Peter and not Peter himself?

- In fact, even in this passage it is not expressly stated that Peter is told anything. On the contrary, **all that had been commanded them they told briefly to those <u>around Peter</u>.**
- Jesus is not reported in the Synoptic Gospels as teaching about 'eternal salvation' – sacred, imperishable or otherwise. We know what his central teaching was and what he preached the most. The word 'salvation' is not mentioned.
- This last sentence is almost certainly a much later addition based on a theology that was later attributed to Jesus rather than anything he taught.

The Longer Ending of Mark

Here is the longer ending.

"Now after he rose early on the first day of the week, he appeared first to Mary Magdalene, from whom he had cast out seven demons. She went and told those who had been with him, while they were mourning and weeping. When they heard that Jesus was alive and had been seen by her, they would not believe it.
Afterward he appeared in another form to two of them as they were walking in the country. And they went back and told the rest; but they did not believe them.
Later he appeared to the eleven themselves as they were sitting at the table; and he upbraided them for their lack of faith and stubbornness, because they had not believed those who saw him after he had risen.

And he said to them, "Go into all the world and proclaim the good news to the whole creation. The one who believes and is baptized will be saved; but whoever does not believe will be condemned. And these signs will accompany those who believe: by using my name they will cast out demons; they will speak in new tongues; they will pick up snakes in their hands; and if they drink any deadly thing, it will not hurt them; they will lay their hands on the sick, and they will get recover."

So then the Lord Jesus after he had spoken to them, was taken up into heaven and sat down at the right hand of God. And they went out and proclaimed the good news everywhere, while the Lord worked with them and confirmed the message by the signs that accompanied it."

Let me repeat - according to the Editors of the New Revised Standard version of the Bible:

'The earliest manuscripts and some other ancient witnesses do not have verses 9–20.
One authority concludes the book with the shorter ending; others include the shorter ending and then continue with verses 9–20. In most authorities, verses 9–20 follow immediately after verse 8, though in some of these authorities the passage is marked as being 'doubtful'.

Perhaps for good reason. And yet – a whole religion has been created on what seems to me to be a somewhat 'doubtful' premise. Without the longer of the two endings, we are left with what might be described as at best an ambiguous position:

- There is <u>perhaps</u> an empty tomb. But it might be that the body is still present.
- There is no resurrection scene. We are simply told that he has been 'raised' and is not 'here'.
- We understand from what Jesus says himself that 'raised' means a spiritual raising as an angel in heaven.
- It is entirely consistent with the teachings of Jesus on the question of resurrection to have a dead physical body with a soul in heaven. Mark 12:24-27.
- There is no prior mention in the Gospel of Mark - of Jesus going to Galilee to be seen.
- There is no mention of Jesus being seen by anyone.
- There is no physical coming back to life as with the instance of the young girl.

The Gospels of Matthew and Luke closely copy with slight variations the version of Mark as described up to verse 8. But both Matthew and Luke to varying degrees add additional verses that mostly shadow the longer ending of Mark.

They write about multiple sightings and meetings with the risen Jesus. It seems odd that the Gospel of Mark which was written the nearest in time to the death of Jesus and which is the primary source of information for

Mathew and Luke does not mention any sightings after Jesus is dead.

An Alternative Explanation of the Miracles

The miracles as they are found in the synoptic gospels are not intended to be descriptions of actual 'physical' events (though they might be), but rather they are at best descriptions of 'spiritual' events. The events can and should be seen as inner spiritual transformations that flow from an individual's metanoia. This is not an unreasonable view.

The Synoptic Gospels do not anywhere mention Jesus teaching as his message or as part of his message a requirement that an individual believe in miracles. This is not part of his call to action. Jesus' primary concern was all people's spiritual well-being.

We have seen that his disciples were instructed to teach 'metanoia' and were 'given authority over unclean spirits'. The disciples were not given the ability to walk on water or cure physical ailments. Their mission as instructed by Jesus was fundamentally concerned spiritual matters only.

Each of the miracle events might more easily be understood once they are accepted as metaphors for the spiritual changes that might be required to enter a higher state of consciousness, the Kingdom of God, the Light, the 99%, Heaven.

Jesus himself tells his disciples that the parable of the sower and other parables are metaphorical. See for example the following passages in Mark: 4:10-24 and 8: 14-21.

In **Matthew 16: 9-11** Jesus makes it clear that yeast is clearly a metaphor.

'Watch out and beware of the yeast of the Pharisees and Sadducees.' ...Do you still not perceive? Do you not remember the five loaves for the five thousand, and how many baskets you gathered? Or the seven loaves for the four thousand, and how many baskets you gathered? How could you fail to perceive that I was not speaking about bread? Beware the yeast of the Pharisees and Sadducees!' Then they understood that he had not told them to beware of the yeast of bread but of the teaching of the Pharisees and Sadducees.

In the light of this, there is no reason to suppose that other events and words set out in the Synoptic Gospels are anything other than allegory or metaphor.

Below is a table with some suggested explanations of the miracles on the basis that these too are metaphors. These are not exhaustive of the many levels of the metaphorical understanding that can be seen in the events. Each of you can add to these suggestions your own understandings.

	Symptom	Metaphor	Cure
1	Blind	Cannot or will not (i.e. refuses) to see - that is, perceive what is being explained	Cured by faith
2	Deaf	Cannot or will not (i.e. refuses) to hear or understand what is being said	Cured by faith
3	Leprosy	An outward expression of inner impurities that are removed by faith. A leper is an outcast of not just human society but God's too. The healing restores and provides an integration back into the Kingdom [of God].	Cured by faith
4	Unclean	A restoration of	Cured by faith

		Spirit	a healthy inner spirit and restoration of at least a basic level of consciousness	
5		Natural Phenomena Bread & Loaves	The hunger is a hunger for spiritual enlightenment and growth	Not only are the thousands satisfied but there is plenty left over for anyone else that also suffers from the same hunger. Again, this is an allegory concerning faith.
6		Walking on Water	The water is a metaphor for Life.	The journey does not have to be like wading through the water. It can be made easier by being above and on top of (i.e. in control of) the turmoil that is

			found in the sea of Life.
7	Resurrection	A lifting up of the consciousness to a higher level	Through faith and a surrendering one's spiritual consciousness can be lifted from a life of darkness into and restored back to Life
8	Lameness	Walking/heading in the wrong direction. The person's ability to walk is to enable them to walk on the right Path	Cured by Faith

What do you believe? In Kabbalah to which we now turn, there are further explanations.

Chapter 9 –
Kabbalah & Jesus

So far in this book we have established that:

1. Jesus existed as an actual and real historical figure. He was a Jew, a Rabbi, and his religion was Judaism as found in the Torah.
2. Jesus himself says that his mission was to simply deliver a message.
3. Jesus was not a Christian.
4. Of the Ten Commandments in the Torah - Jesus declares that the first and most important is to love God. The second is to treat your neighbour as you would like to be treated.
5. The main source of historical information as to what Jesus said and did is found in the Synoptic Gospels.
6. For a number of reasons, we should treat with caution what is said about Jesus in the Synoptic Gospels.
7. The earliest of the Synoptic Gospels to be written was Mark –approximately 20 – 30 years after the death of Jesus. The Gospel of Mark is mostly the source of all materials for the other two Synoptic Gospels – Matthew and Luke.
8. Nevertheless, it is pretty obvious that Jesus was a messenger and his core message is given in all of the three Synoptic Gospels; at

the beginning of each of them. It was very simple.

"Metanoia, for the Kingdom of God has drawn near"

Or as I express it in modern speak:

"Change your attention from earthly matters to spiritual matters - and you will find peace and happiness"

9. That core message of 'metanoia' has been misrepresented by organised religion as a result of a mistranslation of the word to 'repent' and a fundamental misunderstanding as to the role and teaching of Jesus.
10. 'Metanoia' is a call to action. A call to take control by redirecting what it is that we direct our primary attention to. To change to our real purpose in life.
11. All the other teachings of Jesus are directed towards an exposition, an explanation of what this core teaching means and its consequences to us.
12. Our primary aim should be to focus on seeking spiritual growth and not the acquisition of material wealth.
13. We should be looking towards forming a total commitment to God to the exclusion of almost all other considerations. In doing so, we will enter the Kingdom.

14. That Kingdom is described as a spiritual plane - a state of being in complete happiness or harmony with all of God's creation.
15. It is frequently remarked upon that what Jesus taught seemed unlike anything that was being taught. It is repeatedly remarked upon that he had an unknown 'authority' that created awe and wonderment to his listeners.
16. Jesus was renowned as a teacher and as a healer – a miracle worker.
17. One of the main means of conveying his teaching was in parables. Confirming secret and hidden meanings.
18. What Jesus taught was a challenge to the established Jewish religious leaders and what they taught. In the end, he was killed at the behest of the Jewish religious establishment.
19. The resurrection of Jesus was almost certainly by his own criterion - a spiritual event – not a physical restoration of life. It was a spiritual raising up.
20. The central teaching of Jesus is as relevant today as it was when he first proclaimed it.

With these points in mind, we can now turn to see whether any of these things are familiar to the teachings of Kabbalah as I had defined in the introduction.

When looking for signs that what Jesus said and did had any connection to Kabbalah, we are again relying on the Synoptic Gospels – especially the Gospel of Mark. Of course, in doing so, we should again treat the materials with caution for all the reasons I have previously mentioned. We simply do not know whether what looks to be a reference to Kabbalah is because Jesus was a Kabbalist or whether the author(s) of the Gospel was a Kabbalist -or later authors of Kabbalah were versed in the words of Jesus and drew inspiration from them.

Further, if the Zohar and/or the Sefer Yetzirah (either oral or written versions) post-date the life of Jesus; though unlikely, it is at least possible that Kabbalah reflects what Jesus taught - rather than the other way around.

In his book 'The Power of Kabbalah' Yehudi Berg sets out thirteen principles of Kabbalah. But the final principle with which he concludes his book is principle thirteen.

'If you have trouble remembering all the lessons laid out in this book, you will find it reassuring to know that Kabbalah has given us one unique bit of wisdom that contains all the other principles within it. It's a magic secret that goes something like this':

''Love thy neighbour as thyself''

'All the rest is mere commentary.'

In Kabbalah there is a great deal of commentary but at the core of its many and varied teachings and insights is the following:

1. There are two basic realities of existence.

   a. Firstly, there is the 1%, world of Darkness and
   b. Secondly there is the 99%, realm of Light.

2. The 1% is the material world in which many operate on a day-to-day basis. It is a world of darkness, fear and chaos.

3. The 1% represents what we call the 'ego'.

4. Yet everything that a Human Being truly desires may only be found in the 99 per cent realm – the realm of abundance, peace, happiness. It is called the Light.

5. The source of the Light is Ein Sof – the Hebrew word for 'infinite'. So the Light emanates from a source.

6. The emanations of the Light are at different levels like the branches of a tree. This tree is known as the Tree of Life. Each branch can be understood as a different level of consciousness – or state of spiritual being.

7. The root of the Tree of Life is called Malkuth and the very tip of the Tree of Life is called Keter.

213

8. The root (Malkuth) is connected to the earth and is the gateway or entry point to reach all the upper branches – or levels.

9. Each human being should take responsibility for his or her thoughts and actions. We must never blame anyone else.

10. We must be pro-active not reactive. We must seize control of our lives. The primary task for all humans is to love God and thereby connect to the 99% realm of Light - to move ever close to the source of the Light - achieve spiritual enlightenment and to fulfil the task of loving our neighbour as we do ourselves.

11. As obstacles arise - often in interaction with other human beings - they should be seen as opportunities for spiritual growth. They are invitations or opportunities to treat people, as we would like to be treated. This includes forgiving people for their 'wrongs' to us and in return, asking forgiveness of and for our own 'wrongs' to others.

12. Be certain in the whole process that the Light is always available. In other words, have faith in the Light and its power and abundance in all that you do.

13. The Light is available here on earth – right now. It is not only in the world to come.

A great deal of Kabbalah's teaching may be found in the two books that I mentioned in Chapter 4 – the Sefer Yetzirah and the Zohar.

The Zohar text according to Kabbalists is a written record of the discussions between Rabbi bar Shimon Yochai and a small group of his fellow Kabbalists. They discuss the hidden and secret meanings of numerous passages found in the Torah and the lessons of understanding to be drawn from those meanings.

I noted in Chapter 4, that there is controversy concerning the origin of the Zohar but it is right to say that nevertheless, mainstream Judaism does not dispute that the Zohar fairly represents the teachings of Kabbalah. As a source for an understanding of Kabbalah it may therefore be relied upon – subject of course to the various cautions that I explained in Chapter 3.

I use the 2001 version of the Zohar produced by the Kabbalah Centre that was translated into English with commentaries in the [1960s] – albeit with some subsequent revisions. This translated version of the Zohar consists of 21 volumes. Each volume is divided into books and each book contains sections that open with an introduction that explains what is to follow.

Next to the original Aramaic text which is reproduced and below it, is a translation and commentary on that text. I have reproduced extracts from the Zohar in the same way (Chapter 4).

But before turning to the Zohar it is helpful to understand some additional core elements of Kabbalah and these may be found in the Sefer Yetzirah —believed to be the oldest of all of the Kabbalah texts.

The Tree of Life is one of the two trees planted in the Garden of Eden – the other being the Tree of Knowledge of Good and Evil. As you already know, the 'forbidden fruit' that Adam and Eve ate was not from the Tree of Life but from the Tree of Knowledge of God and Evil.

"Out of the ground the Lord God made to grow every tree that is pleasant to the sight and good for food, the tree of life also in the midst of the garden, and the tree of knowledge of good and evil."

[Genesis 2:9]

According to Kabbalah the Light is from the ultimate source of all creation. The Light is the life force that gives birth to human beings, stars and all things – material and spiritual. But note – the Light emanates from God (Ein Sof – the Infinite Being) – but the Light is not Ein Sof. In the same way that Jesus spoke about the Kingdom of God. The 'Kingdom' is not God – but a state of being as a result of being connected to God.

In Kabbalah there are ten spiritual levels. These are known as the Ten Sephirot – the Ten Emanations.

The Ten Sephirot are as follows:

Aramaic Transliteration	Aramaic	English
Keter	כתר	Crown
Chochmah	חכמה	Wisdom
Binah	בינה	Understanding
Da'at	דעת	Knowledge
Zeir Anpin	זעיר אנפי	Small Face
Chesed	חסד	Mercy (Chassadim - plural)
Gvurah	גבורה	Judgment (Gvurot – plural)
Tiferet	תפארת	Splendor
Netzach	נצח	Victory (Eternity)
Hod	הוד	Glory
Yesod	יסוד	Foundation
Malkuth	מלכות	Kingdom

Below is the Ten Sephirot in a diagram. In Kabbalah this diagram represents the **Tree of Life** - the same Tree of Life that is referred to in Beresheet/Genesis in the Torah.

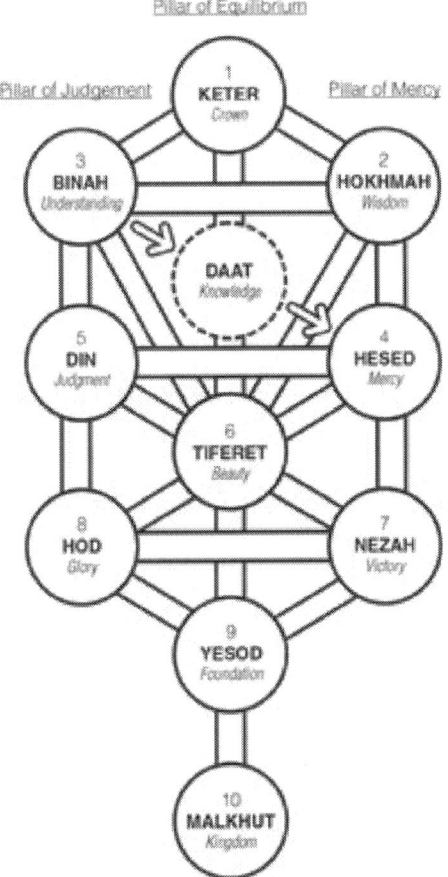

Pillar of Equilibrium

Pillar of Judgement

Pillar of Mercy

1
KETER
Crown

3
BINAH
Understanding

2
HOKHMAH
Wisdom

DAAT
Knowledge

5
DIN
Judgment

4
HESED
Mercy

6
TIFERET
Beauty

8
HOD
Glory

7
NEZAH
Victory

9
YESOD
Foundation

10
MALKHUT
Kingdom

The Ten Emanations are not 'named' in the Sefer Yetzirah in the way shown in the diagram above. This was a later development in Kabbalah and first appears in the Zohar. Each name is derived from the Torah. See [Exodus 31:3 – Proverbs 3:19,20 – Proverbs 24:3,4 – 1 Chronicles 29:11].

The Torah and Kabbalah sees the human soul as mirroring the divine (after Genesis 1:27, "God created man in his own image, in the image of God He created him, male and female He created them"), and more widely, all creations as reflections of their life source in the sephirot. Therefore, the sephirot also describe the spiritual life of man, and constitute the conceptual paradigm in Kabbalah for understanding everything.

This relationship between the soul of man and the divine, gives Kabbalah one of its two central metaphors in describing divinity, alongside the other ohr (Light) metaphor.

Two sephirot (Binah and Malkuth) are feminine, as the female principle in Kabbalah describes a vessel that receives the male light, then inwardly nurtures and gives birth to lower sephirot. Corresponding to this is the female divine presence.

The Kabbalah Tree of Life starts at Malkuth at the bottom and rises all the way up to Keter. The concept of God having both male and female attributes is hardly mentioned (if at all) in Christianity - despite clear references in the Torah.

The Greek word for Kingdom is **Βασιλεία** basileia and this is derived from the Aramaic term 'malkutha' and Hebrew 'malkuth'. As you can see above, the word 'malkuth' means 'Kingdom'. The Tree of Life in Hebrew is עץ חיים Etz Hayim or Etz Chaim.

In Judaism the Tree of Life (Eitz Chaim – transliteration) is sometimes figuratively applied to the Torah and variously in the Book of Proverbs as 'the Torah' [3:18], 'the fruit of a righteous man [11:30], a 'desire fulfilled' and 'healing tongue'.

The point is that in Judaism, the Tree of Life does not take on any mystical reference or use. But we would not expect it to do so for the mystical and spiritual aspect of the Torah may be found in Kabbalah. You will recall that in Chapter 7, I pointed out that the precise phrase:

'Kingdom of God' or 'Kingdom of Heaven'

does not occur as such in the Torah. Indirect reference to the 'Kingdom' of God occurs only once in the Torah whereas it appears over fifty times in the Gospels of Matthew, Mark, Luke and John.

Here is the sole indirect reference in the Torah:

"Yours, O Lord are the **greatness**, the **power**, the **glory**, the **victory**, and the **majesty**: for **all** that is in the heavens and on the earth is yours; yours is the **Kingdom**. O Lord, and you are exalted as head above all."

[1 Chronicles 29:11]

In Kabbalah 'greatness' here is associated with Chesed (mercy) and 'all' with Yesod (foundation'). These too are part of the Tree of Life. Christians will of course be familiar with the response after the Lord's Prayer in the Mass and the Service - without realizing its potential hidden meaning:

"For the <u>Kingdom</u>, the <u>power,</u> and the <u>glory</u> are yours, <u>now</u> and forever"

The phrase 'the Kingdom of God', or its equivalents 'Kingdom of heaven' or Kingdom of my Father' occur in sayings 13 times in the Gospel of Mark and in some 25 sayings in Matthew, 6 sayings in Luke and 13 sayings in Q (the unknown source I referred to in Chapter 3. The point I am making is very simple but may have far reaching implications.

When Jesus talks about the 'Kingdom' of God or the 'Kingdom' of heaven, he is not drawing from something within the Torah. It is something outside of that or hidden within it. Although Malkuth (Kingdom) is part of the Tree of Life, it is the entry point or basic level of spiritual consciousness. It is the root that connects to the trunk and upper branches. However, it is the gateway to all the other and higher levels.

"Enter through the narrow gate; for the gate is wide and the road is easy that leads to destruction, and there are many who take it.

For the gate is narrow and the road is hard that leads to life, and there are few who find it."

[Matthew 7:13 – 14]

In Kabbalah:

- Malkuth (Kingdom) is God's presence on earth. It is in Malkuth (Kingdom) that God's will or energy is made manifest in the physical world. Malkuth (Kingdom) is the physical world around us, the creation of the divine.
- As a result, Malkuth (Kingdom) is the world or earth that we experience, which is filled with the divine presence (Shechinah).
- Malkuth (Kingdom) is that aspect of the divine which is totally immanent, here and now, closer to you even than the concept of you.

The Shechinah I mention above is the divine feminine.

Interestingly one of the additional titles of Malkuth is 'Kalah' which means 'the Bride'.

The parables of the Ten Virgins [Matthew 25: 1] and the Wedding Feast [Matthew 22:1-14] might now be viewed in a different way. (See Chapter 7).

Indeed, once we are aware of the Tree of Life, the Ten Sephirot and the concept of Malkuth (Kingdom), each of the parables of Jesus can take on a different more profound meaning.
The frequent use of seeds, sowing, planting, taking root, growth and branches - all of which are clearly connected with the earth take on a different meaning with clear allusion to the Tree of Life.

In the following passages, I invite you to look back at the various passages in Chapter that I have referred to concerning the miracles and parables. As you do so, you will begin to realise how the metaphors and teachings of Jesus bear striking similarities to the extracts I set out from the Kabbalistic texts. To assist you, I have underlined particular words and phrases.

There is a section of the book Pinchas [B] in the Zohar that explains the nature and importance of Malkuth. Here are some relevant passages:

Original Aramaic

839. אִיהִי שְׁלָמִים, שְׁלִימוּ דִּשְׁמָא דַּיְדֹנָד, בְּכָל דַּרְגָּא וְדַרְגָּא. אִיהִי ה'. אֲדֹנָי. י' דַּיְדֹנָד. אִיהִי ה' מָן אֱלֹהִים. אִיהִי ה' מָן אֶהְיֶה. י' מָן שַׁדַּי. סוֹף דְּכָל הֲוָיָה וְכִנּוּי. ובג"ד אִתְּמַר בָּהּ, סוֹף דָּבָר הַכֹּל נִשְׁמָע אֶת הָאֱלֹהִים יְרָא וְאֶת מִצְוֹתָיו שְׁמוֹר. אִיהִי סוֹף מֵעֶשֶׂר סְפִירָאן, יַם סוֹף. שְׁלִימוּ דְּעֶלְאִין וְתַתָּאִין. אִיהוּ תַּרְעָא לְאַעְלָא לְכָל חָכְמְתָא, לְכָל כִּנּוּי וַהֲוָיָה, וּלְאַעְלָא בְּכָל סְפִירָה וּסְפִירָה, יְדִיעָה דְּכֹלָּא. וּפָחוּת מִינָהּ, לֵית רְשׁוּ לְשׁוּם בִּרְיָה, לְאַשְׁגָּחָא לְשׁוּם יְדִיעָה בָּעוֹלָם. עָלָהּ אִתְּמַר, זֶה הַשַּׁעַר לַיְיָ' צַדִּיקִים יָבֹאוּ בוֹ.

The translation is:

839. <u>And she, MALCHUT</u>, is CALLED '<u>peace offerings</u>' (Heb. *shelamim*) because she is the completion (Heb. *shlemut*) of the Name Yud Hei Vav Hei in each and every grade. She is Hei OF YUD HEI VAV HEI; she is Adonai; she is the Yud of Yud Hei Vav Hei; she is the Hei of Elohim; she is the Hei of Eheyeh. She is the Yud of Shadai: (Shin-Dalet-Yud); she is the end of every Yud Hei Vav Hei and appellative, <u>wherefore it is said about her: "The end of the matter, when all is said and done: Fear Elohim and keep His commandments"</u> (Kohelet 12:13). She is the end (Heb. *sof*) of the ten Sfirot and is called '*Yam Suf*' (Eng. 'the reed sea'). She is the completion of the upper beings and of the lower beings; she is the gate by which one has to enter for all wisdom and for every appellative and Yud Hei Vav Hei and for entering into each and every Sfirah. She is the knowledge of everything, and without NAMELY MALCHUT no creature has permission to look into any knowledge that is in the world. About her it is said: <u>"this is the gate of Hashem, into which the righteous shall enter"</u> (Tehilim 118:20).

[Page 252 para 839]

Original Aramaic

‎840. אִיהוּ שֵׁם מ"ב אַתְוָון, דְּבְהוֹן אִתְבְּרִיאוּ עִלָּאִין וְתַתָּאִין. אִיהִי אִתְקְרִיאַת עַיִן מִסְּטְרָא דְּימִינָא, הֲנֵה עֵין יְדֹוָד אֶל יְרֵאָיו. וְאִתְקְרִיאַת אֹזֶן מִסְּטְרָא דִּשְׂמָאלָא, הַטֵּה אֱלֹהַי אָזְנְךָ וּשֲׁמָע. וְאִתְקְרִיאַת רֵיחַ מִסְּטְרָא דְּעַמּוּדָא דְּאֶמְצָעִיתָא. וְאִתְקְרִיאַת פֶּה, מִגַּרְמָהּ. הה"ד פֶּה אֶל פֶּה אֲדַבֶּר בּוֹ.

The translation is:
840. She, MALCHUT, is the 42-letter Name, NAMELY, THE FOUR LETTERS OF YUD HEI VAV HEI, THE TEN LETTERS OF IT BEING FULLY SPELLED, AND THE 28 LETTERS OF THE FULL SPELLING FULLY SPELLED.

THIS AMOUNTS TO 42 LETTERS, AND MALCHUT IS
THE SECRET OF THE FINAL HEI'S THAT ARE IN THE
42-LETTER NAME, through which the upper and lower
beings were created. She is called 'eye' from the right
side, WHICH IS THE CHOCHMAH IN HER, AS IT IS
WRITTEN: "Behold, the eye of Hashem is upon those
who fear Him" (Tehilim 33:18); and she is called 'ear'
from the left side, WHICH IS THE BINAH IN HER, AS IT
IS WRITTEN: "O my Elohim, incline Your ear, and hear"
(Daniel 9:18). And from the aspect of the Central Pillar,
WHICH IS THE TIFERET IN HER, she is called 'smell,'
while from her own aspect, WHICH IS MALCHUT, she is
called 'mouth,' as it is written: "With him I speak mouth
to mouth" (Bemidbar 12:8).

[Page 252 para 840]

Original Aramaic

841. אִתְקְרִיאַת פְּקוּדָא קַדְמָאָה אָנֹכִי, מִסִּטְרָא דְּכֶתֶר, דְּאִיהוּ אַיִ"ן
מֵאֱלֹהֵינוּ. אָנֹכִי בֵּיהּ כ', כֶּתֶר. וּבֵיהּ אַיִן. וְכֶתֶר אִתְקְרֵי מִסִּטְרָא
דְּאִימָא עִלָּאָה. דְּאִדְכַּר לְגַבָּהּ חַמְשִׁין זִמְנִין יְצִיאַת מִצְרַיִם
בְּאוֹרַיְיתָא. וְאִיהִי ב"ת מִן בְּרֵאשִׁית, דִּכְלִילָא עֲשַׂר אֲמִירָן, מִסִּטְרָא
דְחָכְמָה בַּת י', בְּחָכְמָה יָסַד אָרֶץ. בְּאַבָּא יָסַד בְּרַתָּא. וְאִיהוּ נָתִיב לֹא
יְדָעוֹ עָיִט, דְּכָלִיל לֹ"ב נְתִיבוֹת, דְּאִינּוּן לֹ"ב אֱלֹהִים מִסִּטְרָא דְּאִימָא
עִלָּאָה, דְּאִתְקְרֵי כָּבוֹד. וְכַד אִתְכְּלִילָן בְּבַרְתָּא, אִתְקְרֵי לֹ"ב. וּבְגִין דָּא
כָּבוֹד לְעֵילָא, לֹ"ב לְתַתָּא.

The translation is:

225

841. And she is called 'the first commandment', "I am (Heb. *anochi*)" (Shemot 20:2), NAMELY, THE BEGINNING OF THE DIVINE REVELATION, from the aspect of Keter, that is in her, which is Ayin (Eng. 'nought'), NAMELY, THE LETTERS ALEPH YUD NUN from 'our Elohim' (Aleph- Lamed-Hei-Yud-Nun-Vav), FOR KETER IS CALLED 'NOUGHT' IN THE SENSE OF ABSENCE OF CONCEPTION. *'anochi'* (Aleph Nun Caf Yud) contains the letter Caf that stands for Keter and Aleph Yud Nun (Heb. *ayin*). And Keter is so called from the aspect of supernal Ima, for whom the Exodus from Egypt is mentioned fifty times in the Torah, CORRESPONDING TO THE FIFTY GATES OF BINAH, AND KETER OF MALCHUT IS IN BINAH. And she is a daughter (Heb. *bat* - Bet Tav) from "In the beginning" (Heb. *Beresheet* Bet Resh Aleph Shin Yud Tav), which includes all of the ten sayings BY WHICH THE WORLD WAS CREATED. And from the aspect of Chochmah, she is the daughter of Yud, AS IT IS SAID: "by wisdom founded the earth" (Mishlei 3:19), NAMELY, MALCHUT, WHICH IS CALLED 'EARTH', for Aba, WHICH IS CHOCHMAH, founded the daughter, WHICH IS MALCHUT. And she is "a path which no bird of prey knows" (Iyov 28:7), which is comprised of 32 paths, namely the 32 Names of Elohim from the aspect of supernal Ima that is called 'glory' (Heb. *kavod* = 32). And when they are included in the daughter, WHICH IS MALCHUT, MALCHUT is called heart (Heb. *lev* = 32), and this is why there is glory above and a heart below.

[Page 252 para 841]

226

Original Aramaic

842. וְי' דִּבְרָן אִתְיְיהִיבוּ. חָמֵשׁ בְּלוּחָא חֲדָא, וַחֲמֵשׁ בְּלוּחָא תִּנְיָינָא. אִיהִי כָּלִיל לוֹן, ה' מְכֶּתֶר עַד גְּבוּרָה. וְה' מֵעַמּוּדָא דְּאֶמְצָעִיתָא, עַד בְּרַתָּא. וְאִינּוּן ה' ה'. וְכִי אִית לְמַלְּלָא בַּעֲשָׂרָה פִיּוֹת. אֶלָּא כָּלִיל לוֹן בְּבַת יְחִידָה י' וְאִתְעֲבֵידוּ כֻּלְּהוּ חֲדָא. אוֹף הָכִי ו', אִתְקְרֵי קוֹל, וְלָא אִשְׁתְּמוֹדְעִין בֵּיהּ, עַד דְּאִשְׁתַּתַּף עִם דִּבּוּר. וּבְגִין דָּא, קוֹל דְּבָרִים אַתֶּם שׁוֹמְעִים.

The translation is:

842. And the Ten Commandments were given on <u>two tablets</u>, <u>five</u> on each, and MALCHUT includes them, for they are the <u>five</u> SFIROT from Keter to Gvurah, and the <u>five</u> SFIROT from the Central Pillar, WHICH IS TIFERET to the daughter, WHICH IS MALCHUT. And they are twice Hei. HE ASKS: IF THE TEN COMMANDMENTS ARE FROM THE TEN SFIROT, is it then possible to speak with ten <u>mouths</u>, WITH EACH SFIRAH SPEAKING WITH ITS OWN SPECIAL MOUTH? HE ANSWERS, He included all TEN COMMANDMENTS in the only daughter, WHICH IS MALCHUT, and all of them became one. THUS, THE TEN COMMANDMENTS BECAME INCORPORATED WITHIN MALCHUT. And so it is that Vav, WHICH IS TIFERET, that is called 'voice', <u>cannot be perceived until it joins with speech</u>, WHICH IS MALCHUT. And this is why IT IS WRITTEN: "<u>you heard the voice of the words</u>" (Devarim 4:12), WHERE VOICE ALLUDES TO ZEIR ANPIN AND WORDS TO MALCHUT.

Further passages in this section of the Zohar contain interesting epithets concerning Malkuth that directly cross reference to the parables and teaching of Jesus – all of which have been previously touched upon.

You may recall the frequent references to eyes and seeing, ears and hearing, and to the miracle cures that involved blindness, deafness and dumbness in Chapter 8.

We noted earlier the somewhat surprising reference to Abba by Jesus. In short, Malkuth, the 'Kingdom' is in one sense the most important Sephirot since it is this point at which the physical earth and all creation connects with the non-physical – with the spiritual. It is the point of access at which connection with the Light is made.

But the potential connections between the teaching of Jesus and Kabbalah do not stop here. In the Sefer Yetzirah the Hebrew letters take on a numerical value and particular significance. The opening paragraph of the Sefer Yitzirah says;

"With 32 mystical paths of Wisdom engraved Yah, the Lord of Hosts, the God of Israel the living God, King of the universe...."

[Sefer Yetzirah 1:10]

The next paragraph of the Sefer Yitzirah at 2:2 explains that these 32 paths are manifest as the 10 Sephirot of Nothingness and 22 Foundation Letters of the Hebrew alphabet. The 10 digits are also manifest in the Ten Sephirot – the Ten Emanations. The Hebrew word for paths here is *Netivot* נתיבות a word that occurs rarely in scripture. Much more common is the word *Derekh*. דרכים

As Rabbi Aryeh Kaplan explains - A *'nativ'* on the other hand is a personal route, a path taken by an individual for his personal use. It is a hidden path without markers or signposts, which one must discover on his own and tread by means of his own devices.

The 32 paths of Wisdom are therefore called *Netivot (plural for nativ)* – the private paths travelled by each individual – which each individual must discover for his or herself.

These paths are said to be mystical – in Hebrew *'Peliyot'* פליאות which comes from the root 'Pala' פלא; which has the connotation of being hidden and separated from the world at large. These paths are hidden, concealed and transcendental. The closely related word *'Peleh'* פלא means 'miracle'. A miracle is separated and independent from the laws of the physical world. It is also influenced by hidden forces.

(Kaplan, Sefer Yetzfirah)

In the light of the above it might be worth reminding ourselves of what we noted earlier in this book concerning:

- Jesus referring to the hidden meanings of the parables – even to his disciples. (See Chapter 7)
- Jesus referring to the hidden treasure.
- The miracles performed by Jesus include ones that defy the laws of the physical universe –e.g. walking on water, the five loaves and two fishes etc. (See Chapter 8).

The type of miracle denoted by the word Peleh is specifically one that is achieved by the manipulation of the 32 paths. The methods of manipulation of these paths is one of the important teachings of Sefer Yetzirah. The control over nature may even extend to creating something out of nothing.

"He formed substance out of chaos and made nonexistence into existence
He carved great pillars from air that cannot be grasped
This is a sign [Alef with them all, and all of them with Alef]
He foresees, transforms and makes all that is formed and all that is spoken:
One Name:
A sign for this thing:
Twenty two objects in a single body."

[Sefer Yetzirah 2:6]

According to Rabbi Aryeh Kaplan, what is being described here by 'formation' is a mental act of creation that is then completed by being brought into actual physical existence. This is achieved from an elevated spiritual state; from which all creation is derived. This spiritual state of being produces the ability to transform - actually changing physical things – such as water into wine. Doing so would be a sign of the attainment of the higher spiritual level.

You will recall:

"The Pharisees and Sadducees came, and to test Jesus they asked him to show them a sign from heaven. 2 He answered them, "When it is evening, you say, 'It will be fair weather, for the sky is red.' 3 And in the morning, 'It will be stormy today, for the sky is red and threatening.' You know how to interpret the appearance of the sky, but you cannot interpret the signs of the times. 4 An evil and adulterous generation asks for a sign, but no sign will be given to it except the sign of Jonah." Then he left them and went away" [Matthew 16:1-4]
The reference to The King of the Universe in the Sefer Yetzirah is explained by Rabbi Aryeh Kaplan in this way:

"This is the mode in which God relates to the universe as a king, and it is associated with the

Sefirah Malkhut (Kingship). Of all the Sefirot, this is the only one which comes into direct contact with the lower stages of creation.
The first designations, 'Yah, the Lord of Hosts, God of Israel, the Living God, King of the Universe, thus designate the Ten Sefirot in their downward mode, as they are the source of all creative force."

First and Last

"Ten Sefirot of Nothingness
Their end is imbedded in their beginning and their beginning in their end."

Rabbi Kaplan explains:

'According to most commentaries, the beginning is Keter [See Tree of Life diagram above] (Crown) while the 'end' is Malkhut (Kingship). These are the two end points of the spiritual dimension. In the most basic level, Keter is seen as the concept of 'cause' while Malkhut is the archetype of 'effect'. Since a cause cannot exist without an effect, and effect cannot exist without a cause, the two are independent of each other'.

Is this then what Jesus is referring to when he repeatedly says:

"But many who are first will be last and the last will be first"

232

[Mark 10:31]

Ohr - The Light

As I have already explained, central to Kabbalah is the effort to seek and live in the Light [Ohr].

Original Aramaic

348. וַיֹּאמֶר אֱלֹקִים יְהִי אוֹר וַיְהִי אוֹר, וְדָא אִיהוּ נְהוֹרָא, דִּבְרָא קָדוֹשׁ בָּרוּךְ הוּא בְּקַדְמִיתָא, וְהוּא נְהוֹרָא דְּעֵינָא, וְהוּא נְהוֹרָא דְּאַחֲזֵי קָדוֹשׁ בָּרוּךְ הוּא לְאָדָם קַדְמָאָה. וַהֲוֵי חָזֵי בֵּיהּ, מִסְיָיפֵי עָלְמָא וְעַד סְיָיפֵי עָלְמָא, וְהוּא נְהוֹרָא דְּאַחֲזֵי קָדוֹשׁ בָּרוּךְ הוּא לְדָוִד, וַהֲנָה מְשַׁבַּח וַאֲמַר מָה רַב טוּבְךָ אֲשֶׁר צָפַנְתָּ לִּירֵאֶיךָ, וְהוּא נְהוֹרָא דְּאַחֲזֵי קָדוֹשׁ בָּרוּךְ הוּא לְמֹשֶׁה, וְחָמָא בֵּיהּ, מִגִּלְעָד וְעַד דָּן.

The translation is:

348. "And Elohim said, 'Let there be light;' and there was light" (Beresheet 1:3). This is the light that the Holy One, blessed be He, created at first, and this is the light of the eye (lit. 'sight'). This is the light that the Holy One, blessed be He, showed Adam, and through it Adam saw from one end of the world to the other. And this is the light that the Holy One, blessed be He, showed

233

David, who said in praise, "Oh how great is your goodness, which you laid up for those who fear you..." (Tehilim 31:20). This is the light that the Holy One, blessed be He, used to show Moses, who saw in it THE ENTIRE LAND OF YISRAEL, from Gilad to Dan.

As it is explained in para 351 on p.378- "Everything that begins with "let there be" (Hebrew vayehi) applies to this world and to the world to come."

[Beresheet A - Page 376 – 378]

This theme is developed still further but what it tells us is this:

The Hidden Light of the Creator was stored in the upper level of Binah [See Tree of Life Diagram] where it was set-aside for the righteous of this world. This is the secret of the world to come. The world to come does not refer to a realm that we reach at death, or at any point in the future. The world to come occurs in the present, at the precise moment we transform [metanoia] our nature and create a new world for ourselves. We are included in the righteous whenever we make these spiritual connections. When we connect to or enter Malkuth – the Kingdom, the World to come, heaven - is present here and now.

Is this not the 'egizen' 'come near' or 'is at hand' part of the central teaching of Jesus?

"the Kingdom of God has come near"

234

Is it not encapsulated in the Lord's Prayer?

'Your Kingdom come. Your will be done, on earth as it is in heaven'

Miracles

In the Prologue of the Zohar from passages 161 to 168 Rabbi Shimon discusses the words in Jeremiah 10;

"As among all the wise men of the nations, and in all their Kingdoms, there is none like you"

Original Aramaic

‏161. אֲמַר לֵיהּ רַבִּי אֶלְעָזָר, הַאי קְרָא דִּכְתִיב מִי לֹא
יִרָאֲךָ מֶלֶךְ הַגּוֹיִם כִּי לְךָ יָאֲתָה, מַאי שִׁבְחָא אִיהוּ. אֲמַר
לֵיהּ: אֶלְעָזָר בְּרִי, הַאי קְרָא בְּכַמָּה דּוּכְתֵּי אִתְּמַר, אֲבָל
וַדַּאי לָאו אִיהוּ הָכִי, דִּכְתִיב כִּי בְּכָל חַכְמֵי הַגּוֹיִם וּבְכָל
מַלְכוּתָם, דְּהָא אָתָא לְמִפְתַּח פּוּמָא דְּחַיָּיבִין, דְּחָשְׁבִין
דְּקֻדְשָׁא בְּרוּךְ הוּא לָא יָדַע הִרְהוּרִין וּמַחְשָׁבִין דִּלְהוֹן,
וּבְגִין כָּךְ אִית לְאוֹדְעָא שְׁטוּתָא דִּלְהוֹן. דִּזְמְנָא חֲדָא
אָתָא פִּילוֹסוֹפָא חֲדָא דְּאֻמּוֹת הָעוֹלָם לְגַבָּאי, אֲמַר לִי,
אַתּוּן אָמְרוּן דֶּאֱלָהֲכוֹן שַׁלִּיט בְּכָל רוּמֵי שְׁמַיָּא, כּוּלְהוֹן
חַיָּילִין וּמַשְׁרְיָין לָא אִדְבְּקָן וְלָא יָדְעֵי אֲתַר דִּילֵיהּ. הַאי
קְרָא לָא אַסְגֵּי יְקָרֵיהּ כָּל כָּךְ, דִּכְתִיב כִּי בְּכָל חַכְמֵי

235

הַגּוֹיִם וּבְכָל מַלְכוּתָם מֵאֵין כָּמוֹדֵ. מַאי שְׁקוּלָא דָא
לִבְנֵי נָשָׁא דִי לֵית לוֹן קִיּוּמָא.

The translation is:

161. Rabbi Elazar said to Rabbi Shimon, there is a verse that reads, "Who would not fear You, O King of the nations? For to You it is fitting" (Yirmeyah 10:7). What sort of praise is this? He answered him: Elazar, my son, this verse has been said in many places. And certainly it is not so; ITS MEANING IS NOT A SIMPLE EXPLANATION, because it is written, "For among all the wise men of the nations, and in all their kingdoms, there is none like You" (Ibid.). And this is written as an excuse for the sinners, FOR THOSE who think that the Holy One, blessed be He, is not aware of their plans and their thoughts. And because of this, their folly should be announced in the open. Because once a philosopher of the nation approached me, and said, you claim that your Elohim governs the entire heights of the heavens, and all the heavenly hosts and legions are not able to approach Him, nor do they know His place. But here, this verse does not add a lot to His honour. As it is written, "as among all the wise men of the nations...there is none like You." What kind of a comparison is this, to be compared with human beings who do not have eternal existence?

Para 161 (page 95)

Rabbi Elazar said to him, there is a verse that reads, ''Who would not fear You, O King of the nations? For you it is fitting''...Elazar, present the Bride with a

236

gift!...that the members of the bridal canopy offered her, you may stand before Him'

Para 161 – 168

This is the commentary in respect of these passages:

"The mighty spiritual powers of the Creator are often entrusted to the righteous. Thus Elijah the Prophet and Elisha were given the power to resurrect the dead. Elijah was given the power to stop and start the rain at will. Joshua was able to stop the sun. The secret revealed by the Zohar pertains to the will of the Creator, and to His intention that we ourselves should have the power to generate miracles.

The Kabbalists teach us that God does not perform miracles, only man does.

It is only our lack of spiritual knowledge of the supernal secrets that prevent us from performing miraculous deeds each day of our lives. Perhaps the most powerful secret for overcoming the limits of nature involves our transformation beyond the tendencies of human nature. When we bring abut a miracle – that is, a dramatic spiritual change – within our inner character, the Upper Worlds mirror our actions. They direct supernal forces into our mundane world, and wondrous acts are accomplished."

As we saw in Chapter 8, what is described here is the essence of what Jesus was teaching. How many times do we read that the healing and miracles are not performed by Jesus or God – but the person's faith or belief? Spiritual transformation arises from **metanoia** - and then miracles arise from faith – which is a total acceptance of or surrendering to God – and with that a connection to the Upper Worlds of the Sephirot.

In the book Beresheet A of the Zohar at paragraph 334 at page 366 we read:

Original Aramaic

334. אֶל הַכָּבוֹד הִרְעִים, כד"א וְרַעַם גְּבוּרוֹתָיו מִי
יִתְבּוֹנֵן, דָּא סִטְרָא דְּאַתְיָא מִן גְּבוּרָה וְנַפְקָא מִנֵּיהּ. דָּבָר
אַחֵר, אֵ"ל הַכָּבוֹד הִרְעִים, דָּא יָמִינָא, דְּנַפְקָא מִנֵּיהּ
שְׂמָאלָא, ה' עַל מַיִם רַבִּים, ה' דָּא חָכְמָה עִלָּאָה דְּאִקְרֵי
יו"ד. עַל מַיִם רַבִּים, עַל הַהוּא עוֹמְקָא סְתִימָאָה דְּנָפִיק
מִנֵּיהּ. כד"א וּשְׁבִילְךָ בְּמַיִם רַבִּים.

Translation

334. **A DIFFICULTY WAS RAISED REGARDING** "The El of glory thunders," **BECAUSE THE TERM EL ALLUDES TO CHESED, WHILE THUNDER IS AN ACTION OF GVURAH. HE SAID THAT** this is according to what is written: "But the thunder of His power who can understand?" (Iyov 26:14). This aspect is revealed by gazing on the thunder of Gvurah that originates in it. **IN OTHER WORDS, THE PHRASE, "THE EL OF**

238

GLORY," IS THE SECRET OF CHESED THAT IS
REVEALED BECAUSE OF GVURAH, AS LIGHT'S
SUPERIORITY OVER DARKNESS. THEREFORE IT IS
WRITTEN: "THE EL OF GLORY THUNDERS,"
BECAUSE IT WAS REVEALED BY GVURAH THROUGH
THUNDER. Another explanation of THE PHRASE "The
El of glory thunders" is that it is THE SECRET OF the
right – WHICH IS CHESED – from which the left—
GVURAH – comes forth, AS THE SFIROT ISSUE AND
EMANATE FROM ONE ANOTHER, AS IS KNOWN.
ACCORDING TO THIS, "THE EL OF GLORY," WHICH IS
CHESED, THUNDERS – EMANATES GVURAH – WHICH
IS THE SECRET OF THUNDER. "Hashem is upon many
waters," means that Hashem is THE REVELATION OF
supernal Chochmah, which is called *Yud* - NAMELY
THAT THE MOCHIN OF THE SUPERNAL ABA AND IMA
is "upon many waters." IT IS REVEALED over that
hidden source from which it emerged, as it is written:
"And Your path in the great waters" (Tehilim 77:20).

According to Kabbalah:

"The voice of Hashem is a supernal secret. It refers to
the process by which the Creator sends forth His
energy and Light into our physical universe. The
word water is a code referring to the Light itself"

(Zohar 1, Beresheet A, Page 365)

In light of the above and what we have discovered in the
Sefer Yetzirah, perhaps the 'miracle' of Jesus walking on
the water, stilling the storm, the miracles of the loaves

and fishes (and other similar events) – all of which involve the manipulation of and being in control of nature - might now be seen in a different way and more easily understood.

Finally, In Beresheet A of the Zohar at paragraphs 232 – 251 the return of Moses in the End of Days is discussed.

To Kabbalists the End of Days is our current era – the age of Aquarius. Here is a synopsis to the above referred passages which are too long to set out here:

"Alongside Moses are two Messiahs: Messiah who is the son of Joseph and Messiah who is the son of David. The Kabbalists teach that the Messiah is not someone whom we passively await. Rather, the word Messiah refers to our own individual spiritual growth, we must achieve aspects of the Messiah within ourselves in order to accelerate the arrival of the Global Messiah. Recognition of this truth – together with love for others and a strong connection to the Aramaic words of the Zohar – will hasten the arrival of the Messiah, universal peace, and immortality."

(Zohar 1, Beresheet A, Page 293)

With all of the above in mind, we might remind ourselves of the way in which I explained in earlier Chapters that, in relation to Jesus;

- Those listening to him were astounded by his teaching and what he did.
- The listeners specifically mention that he speaks and acts with an unknown or 'hidden' 'authority'.
- It is clear that the source of the 'authority' is not immediately obvious in the Torah.
- He was asked to provide a sign to prove his credentials as a prophet.
- The listeners are perplexed as to the source of his 'authority'.
- He speaks in parables – where the meaning of the path to and understanding of the Kingdom - is hidden.
- He repeatedly remarks that people do not 'see' or 'hear' his message.
- He repeatedly helps people cure themselves of illnesses that involves sight, hearing and speaking. But it is faith that really brings about the change.
- He uses the word 'Aba' to refer to the 'person' to who prayers should be addressed.
- He explains that the Kingdom is not at a future place or date. He explains that the Kingdom is near at hand – it is available now – in the present.
- He exhorts everyone to turn their attention towards the Kingdom and to God – the King.
- He does not claim to be the Messiah – simply a messenger of the good news;

'Metanoia, the Kingdom of God has come near'

or in modern parlance;

"Change the emphasis of your energy and attention from Earthly matters to Spiritual matters - and you will find peace and happiness"

Chapter 10 –
Messiah

It has always struck me that in declaring Jesus as the Messiah there are two fundamental underlying assumptions:

1. Firstly - The Judaic concept of the Messiah is correct in the first place.
2. Secondly - Jesus fulfilled the Judaic requirements of the Messiah.

As with all major organised religions there is no consensus on all matters and that is true of Judaism also. Indeed, as we have already seen, when Jesus was preaching his simple message, there were a number of 'branches' or sects of the Jewish religion (Pharisees, Essenes, Sadducees) with each having different views on some fundamental issues.

In Judaism the word Messiah is 'Mashiac' which when transliterated into Greek and then English means simply 'anointed' or 'covered in oil'. The concept of a Messiah is not expressly mentioned in the first five books of the Torah. Nevertheless, it forms part of the Judaic tradition going back long before the birth of Jesus.

In traditional Judaism, the anointed one or the Messiah, will have at least the following attributes:

1. He will be a King – an earthly King
2. He will be a descendant of King David
3. He will be anointed with holy anointing oil – as part of his coronation ceremony
4. He will rule the Jewish people during an age of peace and brotherhood for all humans – not just Jews.

In fact, the Torah points to the Messiah having a number of additional qualities in order to qualify as the Messiah. Many of the scriptural requirements concerning the Messiah, what he will do, and what will be done during his reign are found in the Book of Isaiah, although Messianic 'requirements' are mentioned by other prophets as well.

Views on whether the Torah passages are Messianic, may vary from and among scholars of ancient Israel, looking at their meaning in original context and from and among rabbinical scholars. Here is a non-exhaustive list of references in Isaiah and other prophets to what might be expected to happen when the Messiah arrives.

Book	Chapter/Verse
Isaiah	32:1-20, 42:1-4, 1:26, 2:4, 2:11-17, 11:1-4, 11:6-12, 26:19, 51:3, 51:11, 52:7, 52:13.
Daniel	9:24-27, 11:2-45, 12:1-12
Zechariah	8:1-13, 12:1-14, 14:1-20
Ezekiel	37:22-23

Depending upon the version of Judaism one follows, what is expected in consequence of the arrival of the Messiah varies. There is no consensus. To demonstrate the diversity and lack of centrality here is a list of some of some of the denominations of Judaism with each having differing views on the Messiah;

- Orthodox
- Hassidic
- Reform and Reconstructionist
- Chabad Messianism
- Conservative Judaism

But despite the differences, it is interesting to note that it is at no time contemplated that the Messiah will be divine – that is to say God – or the Son of God. In Judaism therefore, the word 'mashiach' refers to the one who is anointed as a king in the end of days. It does not mean 'saviour'. It means anointed. The Latin word for anointed is 'christos', from which we get Christ and thus Christian.

The anointing referred to above is the same as when Elizabeth II, the current Queen of the United Kingdom was anointed as Queen. It is meant as a symbolic recognition not of the Queen's divinity but of the fact that her appointment is made and approved by God.

This is the idea of 'Dieu et Mon Droit' as mentioned in the Introduction.

The concept of 'saviour' is nothing to do with the Judaic concept of an anointed king. It is something that developed as part of Christianity theology – long after the death of Jesus.

In the Synoptic Gospels, Jesus did not say in terms 'I am the Saviour' and nor did he say in terms 'I am the Messiah'.

At best he is reported as answering in the affirmative the question 'Are you the Messiah?' But whether he really gave an affirmative answer might reasonably be called into doubt when we look more closely at what he is reported as saying and the context.

Here are the reported responses to the question 'Are you the Messiah?' (in the Synoptic Gospels):

'I am'

[Mark 14:61-62]

You have said so'

[Matthew 26:64]

'If I tell you, you will not believe'

[Luke 22:67]

The response given by Jesus when asked by the chief priests and scribes if he was 'the Son of God' is reported in Luke as being:

'You say that I am'

[Luke 22:70]

This response of 'you say so' has been interpreted by some scholars (especially those affiliated with Christian Churches) as being the equivalent of 'yes'.

In other words, whilst Jesus is never reported as saying 'I am the Messiah' – when questioned, he does not deny that he claims to be the Messiah and in fact effectively says 'yes' he is. In Mark of course, he is reported as saying 'I am' in clear terms. But it is interesting to note that when asked by Pontious Pilate if he was the 'King of the Jews', he is reported in each of the Synoptic Gospels as replying:

'You say so'.

[Mark 15: 2, Matthew 27:11 and Luke 23: 3]

Are we really to believe that Jesus was claiming to be the King of the Jews – an earthly King as opposed to a purely spiritual King? Based on the logic described above we are compelled to do so. But that is clearly not correct.

It is also clear from each of the Synoptic Gospels, that Pilate did not believe Jesus to be the King of the Jews - despite Jesus purportedly claiming that he was.

We have then the following position:

- Jesus is never reported as saying to anyone 'I am the Messiah'
- Jesus is never reported as saying 'I am the Saviour'.
- The word 'Christ' simply means anointed – as in an earthly King.
- In only one of the three Synoptic Gospels [Mark] does Jesus claim in clear terms by the use of the words 'I am' to be the Messiah.
- Mark is the earliest of the three Synoptic Gospels. It seems strange that Matthew and Luke did not repeat such a clear answer to such an important question.
- The phrase 'you say so' or its equivalent may be the same as a 'yes'. If it is to be interpreted in this way, then it should then be understood that Jesus also claimed to be the 'King of the Jews'.
- So far as I am aware no Christian religions of any denomination has ever claimed Jesus to be a temporal, earthly King.

The balance of the evidence produced above from the Synoptic Gospels would not point to Jesus ever claiming to be the Messiah.

But as I shall now explain, there are further reasons why we might consider with exceptional caution what Mark reports Jesus as saying.

Even assuming for a moment that the prophesy of the Messiah of Judaism (an anointed king) is correct – [and that is an article of faith] – then it should by now be obvious that Jesus – a Jewish Rabbi who taught a simple message – did not meet the criteria that he himself as a practicing Jew would have expected. According to original Christianity – that is to say the disciples and followers of Jesus during his life and shortly after his death:

1. Jesus was or rather is the Messiah of Judaism; and as a result
2. The crucifixion of Jesus began the period of peace and brotherhood referred to above.

Again, by the criteria of Judaism and the criteria of the early Christians - Jesus was not the Messiah.

In fact, the first Christians – nearly all of whom were Jews - began to realise that what they originally thought was an imminent fulfilment of the arrival of the Messiah (as laid out in the Torah) in the person of Jesus did not materialise and would be delayed.

Firstly, Jesus was crucified. He was dead. How could he lead as a King – anointed or otherwise?

Moreover, what followed his death was anything but a time of peace. In fact, within a short period of time following the death of Jesus, outright insurrection and war broke out between the Jews and the Romans, culminating in the complete destruction of the Temple in Jerusalem in AD 70, the death of tens of thousands of Jews and the scattering of the Jews who fled for their lives, creating one of the largest and longest diaspora in human history.

Things did not improve for Jews, who did not return to the Land of Israel and gain full independence as a recognised state until 1948.

Israel has been in a state of war almost continuously ever since.

As a result of Jesus' failure to meet the criteria of the Jewish Messiah, the Christians who began to count Gentiles (non-Jews) among them, began to formulate a new concept – a concept that is not found in the Torah. It is called - the 'parousia' - the second coming of Jesus (not anyone else mind you).

But let us look at the context in which Jesus is asked whether he is the Messiah.

The references above concerning Jesus' answer to the question 'Are you the Messiah' are taken from what is reported of the trial of Jesus before the Sanhedrin and Pontius Pilate.

Although it is not possible to be absolutely certain, it would appear that the claim to be the one chosen by God as the mashiach (Messiah), was less significant than the claim to divinity, which ostensibly caused the high priest's horrified accusation of blasphemy and the subsequent call for the death sentence.

Before Pilate, on the other hand, it was merely the assertion of his claim to be royal in an earthly sense, that purportedly gave grounds for concern.

But how reliable is this passage in Mark? There must be at least some material doubt as to the authenticity of what was said and occurred.

1. Who was present at the cross examination of Jesus other than the high priest, the chief priests, the elders and the scribes - the Sanhedrin?
2. Who was the person that observed the scene as it happened and then later told Jesus followers? If we are to believe the rest of the narrative in Mark – all of the disciples had fled for their lives. Even or especially Peter (his most trusted and loyal).
3. Who among the disciples of Jesus would have been allowed to be present at a meeting of the Sanhedrin? We are never directly told.
4. Jesus had not until this hearing before the Sanhedrin claimed to be the Messiah or divine.
5. Why would Jesus now claim to be the Messiah?
6. Why would Jesus now claim to be divine in the way that the Chief Rabbi of the Sanhedrin puts it to him? In the context of Jesus being a Rabbi it is

absolutely absurd to think that he would have made such a claim.

7. Throughout the Synoptic Gospels - Jesus himself only ever publically claimed to be 'the Son of Man' – a phrase that essentially means 'an ordinary bloke'. The exact opposite of the divine.

A reasonable explanation might be that these passages were later insertions by Christians who sought to substantiate their (mistaken) belief that Jesus was the Messiah. But perhaps there is another explanation as I shall explain in the final chapter of this book.

What is apparent however, from the fact that Jesus was referred to the Roman authorities at all and eventually crucified, is that he had clearly done some 'wrong doing' that upset the Jewish Religious Establishment.

There are many reports in the Synoptic Gospels of Jesus challenging and offending the priest and scribes by what he said and did.

For example:

"Now some of the scribes were sitting there, questioning in their hearts, "Why does this fellow speak in this way? It is blasphemy! Who can forgive sins but God alone?" **At once Jesus perceived in his spirit that they were discussing these questions among themselves; and he said to them, "Why do you raise such questions in your hearts? Which is easier, to say to the paralytic, 'Your sins are forgiven,' or to**

say, 'Stand up and take your mat and walk'? But so
that you may know that the <u>Son of Man</u> has authority
on earth to forgive sins"—he said to the paralytic—
"I say to you, stand up, take your mat and go to your
home." And he stood up, and immediately took the
mat and went out before all of them; so that they
were all amazed and glorified God, saying, "We have
never seen anything like this!"

[Mark 2:6-12]

"And as he sat at dinner in Levi's house, many tax
collectors and sinners were also sitting with Jesus and
his disciples—for there were many who followed him.
When the scribes of the Pharisees saw that he was
eating with sinners and tax collectors, they said to his
disciples, <u>"Why does he eat with tax collectors and
sinners?"</u> When Jesus heard this, he said to them,
"Those who are well have no need of a physician, but
those who are sick; I have come to call not the
righteous but sinners."

[Mark 2:15-17]

"One Sabbath he was going through the grain fields;
and as they made their way his disciples began to
pluck heads of grain. The Pharisees said to him,
<u>"Look, why are they doing what is not lawful on the
Sabbath?"</u> And he said to them, "Have you never
read what David did when he and his companions
were hungry and in need of food? He entered the
house of God, when Abiathar was high priest, and ate

the bread of the Presence, which it is not lawful for any but the priests to eat, and he gave some to his companions." Then he said to them, "The Sabbath was made for humankind, and not humankind for the Sabbath; so the Son of Man is lord even of the Sabbath."

[Mark 2: 23 -28]

Again he entered the synagogue, and a man was there who had a withered hand. They watched him to see whether he would cure him on the Sabbath, so that they might accuse him. And he said to the man who had the withered hand, "Come forward." Then he said to them, "Is it lawful to do good or to do harm on the Sabbath, to save life or to kill?" But they were silent. He looked around at them with anger; he was grieved at their hardness of heart and said to the man, "Stretch out your hand." He stretched it out, and his hand was restored. The Pharisees went out and immediately conspired with the Herodians against him, how to destroy him.

[Mark 3: 1-6]

We cannot know whether the event described above came after the ones previously cited. We cannot know that the Pharisees conspired against Jesus to destroy him or that this event is the trigger. But what we are being told in each of these passages is that Jesus was clearly challenging the established 'norm'. He continues to do so.

"When his family heard it, they went out to restrain him, for people were saying, "He has gone out of his mind." And the scribes who came down from Jerusalem said, "He has Beelzebul, and by the ruler of the demons he casts out demons." And he called them to him, and spoke to them in parables, "How can Satan cast out Satan? If a Kingdom is divided against itself, that Kingdom cannot stand. And if a house is divided against itself, that house will not be able to stand. And if Satan has risen up against himself and is divided, he cannot stand, but his end has come. But no one can enter a strong man's house and plunder his property without first tying up the strong man; then indeed the house can be plundered."

[Mark 3: 22-27]

Speaking in parables seems to be the means by which Jesus indirectly makes his challenge. He is hiding the true purport of what he is saying behind an apparently innocuous story. Deeply embedded in the words are a more telling, hidden truth.

"When he was alone, those who were around him along with the twelve asked him about the parables. And he said to them, "To you has been given the secret of the Kingdom of God, but for those outside, everything comes in parables; in order that 'they may indeed look, but not perceive, and may indeed listen, but not understand;

255

so that they may not turn again and be forgiven.'"
And he said to them, "Do you not understand this
parable? Then how will you understand all the
parables? The sower sows the word. These are the
ones on the path where the word is sown: when they
hear, Satan immediately comes and takes away the
word that is sown in them. And these are the ones
sown on rocky ground: when they hear the word,
they immediately receive it with joy. But they have no
root, and endure only for a while; then, when trouble
or persecution arises on account of the word,
immediately they fall away. And others are those
sown among the thorns: these are the ones who hear
the word, but the cares of the world, and the lure of
wealth, and the desire for other things come in and
choke the word, and it yields nothing. And these are
the ones sown on the good soil: they hear the word
and accept it and bear fruit, thirty and sixty and a
hundredfold."

[Mark 4: 10-20]

Those who are listening and seeing what he is saying
from his perspective will see, hear and understand what
is really being said. However, his messages did not
always deliver in such an understated way; at times he
made his criticisms very clear.

"Now when the Pharisees and some of the scribes
who had come from Jerusalem gathered around him,
they noticed that some of his disciples were eating

with defiled hands, that is, without washing them. (For the Pharisees, and all the Jews, do not eat unless they thoroughly wash their hands, thus observing the tradition of the elders; and they do not eat anything from the market unless they wash it; and there are also many other traditions that they observe, the washing of cups, pots, and bronze kettles. So the Pharisees and the scribes asked him, "Why do your disciples not live according to the tradition of the elders, but eat with defiled hands?" He said to them, "Isaiah prophesied rightly about you hypocrites, as it is written,
'This people honours me with their lips,
but their hearts are far from me;
in vain do they worship me,
teaching human precepts as doctrines.'
You abandon the commandment of God and hold to human tradition."

[Mark 7: 1-8]

"Then he said to them, "You have a fine way of rejecting the commandment of God in order to keep your tradition! For Moses said, 'Honour your father and your mother'; and, 'Whoever speaks evil of father or mother must surely die.' But you say that if anyone tells father or mother, 'Whatever support you might have had from me is Corban' (that is, an offering to God then you no longer permit doing anything for a father or mother, thus making void the word of God through your tradition that you have handed on. And you do many things like this."

[Mark 7: 9-13]

These are direct criticisms. Here he is talking to the same Pharisees. He continues:

"Then he called the crowd again and said to them, "Listen to me, all of you, and understand: 15 <u>there is nothing outside a person that by going in can defile, but the things that come out are what defile.</u>"

[Mark 7:14]

We are seeing a pattern here of Jesus extending and explaining the Torah in a new way.

"When he had left the crowd and entered the house, his disciples asked him about the parable. He said to them, "Then do you also fail to understand? Do you not see that whatever goes into a person from outside cannot defile, since it enters, not the heart but the stomach, and goes out into the sewer?" (Thus he declared all foods clean.) And he said, "It is what comes out of a person that defiles. <u>For it is from within, from the human heart, that evil intentions come: fornication, theft, murder, adultery, avarice, wickedness, deceit, licentiousness, envy, slander, pride, folly. All these evil things come from within, and they defile a person.</u>"

[Mark 7: 17-23]

This is new teaching.

"Now the disciples had forgotten to bring any bread;
and they had only one loaf with them in the boat. And
he cautioned them, saying, <u>"Watch out—beware of
the yeast of the Pharisees and the yeast of Herod."</u>
They said to one another, "It is because we have no
bread." And becoming aware of it, Jesus said to
them, "Why are you talking about having no bread?
<u>Do you still not perceive or understand? Are your
hearts hardened? Do you have eyes, and fail to see?
Do you have ears, and fail to hear? And do you not
remember? When I broke the five loaves for the five
thousand, how many baskets full of broken pieces did
you collect?" They said to him, "Twelve." "And the
seven for the four thousand, how many baskets full of
broken pieces did you collect?" And they said to him,
"Seven." Then he said to them, "Do you not yet
understand?"</u>

[Mark 8:14-21]

As we have already seen in Chapter 8, the numbers
twelve (12) and seven (7) have a significance in
Kabbalah. They are not chosen randomly.

"<u>Some Pharisees came, and to test him</u> they asked,
"Is it lawful for a man to divorce his wife?" He
answered them, "What did Moses command you?"
They said, "Moses allowed a man to write a
certificate of dismissal and to divorce her." But Jesus

said to them, **"Because of your hardness of heart he wrote this commandment for you.**

But from the beginning of creation, 'God made them male and female.' 'For this reason a man shall leave his father and mother and be joined to his wife, and the two shall become one flesh.' So they are no longer two, but one flesh. Therefore what God has joined together, let no one separate."
Then in the house the disciples asked him again about this matter. He said to them, "Whoever divorces his wife and marries another commits adultery against her; and if she divorces her husband and marries another, she commits adultery."

Whilst I have emphasised the conflict element of the above passage, of particular interest is when Jesus says:

"But from the beginning of creation, 'God made them male and female".

Here again, we have an interesting connection with Kabbalah and what we saw it teaches with respect to The Tree of Life.

The Tree of Life includes a declaration of the Male and Female element of all creation. You will recall that Kabbalah sees the human soul as mirroring the divine (after Genesis 1:27, "God created man in His own image, in the image of God He created him, male and female He created them"), and more widely, all creations as reflections of their life source in the sephirot.

But returning to the conflict and confrontation between Jesus and the Establishment:

"**Again they came to Jerusalem**. As he was walking in the temple, the chief priests, the scribes, and the elders came to him and said, "**By what authority are you doing these things? Who gave you this authority to do them?**" Jesus said to them, "I will ask you one question; answer me, and I will tell you by what authority I do these things. Did the baptism of John come from heaven, or was it of human origin? Answer me." They argued with one another, "If we say, 'From heaven,' he will say, 'Why then did you not believe him?' But shall we say, 'Of human origin'?"—they were afraid of the crowd, for all regarded John as truly a prophet. So they answered Jesus, "We do not know." And Jesus said to them, "**Neither will I tell you by what authority I am doing these things.**"

[Mark 11:27 – 33]

But eventually, the meaning behind the parables becomes obvious:

"**Then he began to speak to them in parables.** "A man planted a vineyard, put a fence around it, dug a pit for the wine press, and built a watchtower; then he leased it to tenants and went to another country. When the season came, he sent a slave to the tenants to collect from them his share of the produce of the

261

vineyard. But they seized him, and beat him, and sent him away empty-handed. And again he sent another slave to them; this one they beat over the head and insulted. Then he sent another, and that one they killed. And so it was with many others; some they beat, and others they killed. 6 He had still one other, a beloved son. Finally he sent him to them, saying, 'They will respect my son.' But those tenants said to one another, 'This is the heir; come, let us kill him, and the inheritance will be ours.' So they seized him, killed him, and threw him out of the vineyard. What then will the owner of the vineyard do? He will come and destroy the tenants and give the vineyard to others. Have you not read this scripture:
'The stone that the builders rejected
has become the cornerstone;
this was the Lord's doing,
and it is amazing in our eyes'?"
<u>When they realized that he had told this parable against them, they wanted to arrest him</u>, but they feared the crowd. So they left him and went away"

[Mark 12:12]

But it is not long before the traps are laid.

<u>"Then they sent to him some Pharisees and some Herodians to trap him in what he said.</u> And they came and said to him, "Teacher, we know that you are sincere, and show deference to no one; for you do not regard people with partiality, but teach the way

of God in accordance with truth. Is it lawful to pay taxes to the emperor, or not? Should we pay them, or should we not?" But knowing their hypocrisy, he said to them, "Why are you putting me to the test? Bring me a denarius and let me see it." And they brought one. Then he said to them, "Whose head is this, and whose title?" They answered, "The emperor's." Jesus said to them, "Give to the emperor the things that are the emperor's, and to God the things that are God's." And they were utterly amazed at him."

[Mark 12: 13-17]

"Some Sadducees, who say there is no resurrection, came to him and asked him a question, saying, "Teacher, Moses wrote for us that if a man's brother dies, leaving a wife but no child, the man shall marry the widow and raise up children for his brother. There were seven brothers; the first married and, when he died, left no children; and the second married the widow and died, leaving no children; and the third likewise; none of the seven left children. Last of all the woman herself died. In the resurrection[d] whose wife will she be? For the seven had married her."
Jesus said to them, "Is not this the reason you are wrong, that you know neither the scriptures nor the power of God? For when they rise from the dead, they neither marry nor are given in marriage, but are like angels in heaven. And as for the dead being raised, have you not read in the book of Moses, in the

story about the bush, how God said to him, 'I am the God of Abraham, the God of Isaac, and the God of Jacob'? He is God not of the dead, but of the living; you are quite wrong."

[Mark 12:18-27]

This is not exactly diplomatic language. By now we are told in Mark that several different groups have sought to question and trap Jesus. What is interesting is that each time he answers, he extends the teaching of the Torah and he rebukes them in no uncertain terms. And it continues.

"While Jesus was teaching in the temple, he said,
"How can the scribes say that the Messiah is the son of David? David himself, by the Holy Spirit, declared,
'The Lord said to my Lord,
"Sit at my right hand,
until I put your enemies under your feet."'
David himself calls him Lord; so how can he be his son?" And the large crowd was listening to him with delight."

[Mark 12: 35-37]

"As he taught, he said, "Beware of the scribes, who like to walk around in long robes, and to be greeted with respect in the marketplaces, and to have the best seats in the synagogues and places of honour at banquets! They devour widows' houses and for the

sake of appearance say long prayers. They will receive the greater condemnation."

[Mark12: 38-41]

Not surprisingly, those who were subjected to his criticism were upset.

"It was two days before the Passover and the festival of Unleavened Bread. The chief priests and the scribes were looking for a way to arrest Jesus by stealth and kill him; for they said, "Not during the festival, or there may be a riot among the people."

[Mark 14:1-2]

"Then Judas Iscariot, who was one of the twelve, went to the chief priests in order to betray him to them. When they heard it, they were greatly pleased, and promised to give him money. So he began to look for an opportunity to betray him"

[Mark 14:10-11]

Eventually as is the way of the world, the Establishment arrested him. What then happens should as I have previously indicated, be treated with some caution. The source of the information is not really clear and anyway the allegations fly in the face of the evidence within the Synoptic Gospels themselves.

We can never know.

"They took Jesus to the high priest; and all the chief priests, the elders, and the scribes were assembled. Peter had followed him at a distance, right into the courtyard of the high priest; and he was sitting with the guards, warming himself at the fire. Now the chief priests and the whole council were looking for testimony against Jesus to put him to death; but they found none. For many gave false testimony against him, and their testimony did not agree. Some stood up and gave false testimony against him, saying, "We heard him say, 'I will destroy this temple that is made with hands, and in three days I will build another, not made with hands.'" But even on this point their testimony did not agree. Then the high priest stood up before them and asked Jesus, "Have you no answer? What is it that they testify against you?" But he was silent and did not answer. Again the high priest asked him, "Are you the Messiah, the Son of the Blessed One?" Jesus said, "I am; and
'you will see the Son of Man
seated at the right hand of the Power,'
and 'coming with the clouds of heaven.'"
Then the high priest tore his clothes and said, "Why do we still need witnesses? You have heard his blasphemy! What is your decision?" All of them condemned him as deserving death. Some began to spit on him, to blindfold him, and to strike him, saying to him, "Prophesy!" The guards also took him over and beat him."

[Mark 14:53-65]

266

The clear implication to be drawn from this passage is that Jesus is found guilty of blasphemy - that is to say speaking sacrilegiously, without appropriate respect about God and/or Judaism.

In Judaism the only blasphemy punishable by death is blaspheming the Ineffable Name. Ineffable means that the 'name' is too great to express. In this context the name referred to is the word for God.

For Jesus to be found guilty of speaking without respect about the ineffable name he would have had to have said something particularly onerous concerning God and in particular his name. Where is there evidence of that?

Jesus does not say the ineffable word for God. That word is YHWH (Yahweh). He did not apparently say anything disrespectful to the name, or in the name of God. But note also, that neither the Chief Priest nor the Sanhedrin and those gathered condemned Jesus to death. They are reported as saying that he was 'deserving of death'. Again, we must view with a sceptical eye the accuracy of what is reported here since it seems clear that none of the followers of Jesus were present.

"As soon as it was morning, the chief priests held a consultation with the elders and scribes and the whole council. They bound Jesus, led him away, and handed him over to Pilate. Pilate asked him, "Are you the King of the Jews?" He answered him, "You say so." Then the chief priests accused him of many

things. Pilate asked him again, "Have you no answer? See how many charges they bring against you." But Jesus made no further reply, so that Pilate was amazed."

[Mark 15: 1-5]

Who was present at this interview to be able to report it in such detail? It being noted of course that the allegation presented to Pilate is not that Jesus had blasphemed – but that according to the Sanhedrin – Jesus claimed to be the King of the Jews. He was presented as a political threat. In the circumstances and not forgetting the caution with which we must accept the accuracy of the passage, even Pilate is incredulous of such an allegation. He apparently knows the underlying reason.

"Then he answered them, "Do you want me to release for you the King of the Jews?" For he realized that it was out of jealousy that the chief priests had handed him over. But the chief priests stirred up the crowd to have him release Barabbas for them instead. Pilate spoke to them again, "Then what do you wish me to do[a] with the man you call the King of the Jews?" They shouted back, "Crucify him!" Pilate asked them, "Why, what evil has he done?" But they shouted all the more, "Crucify him!" So Pilate, wishing to satisfy the crowd, released Barabbas for them; and after flogging Jesus, he handed him over to be crucified"

[Mark 15:10 -15].

Quite how the author of Mark knew what Pilate thought is of course a mystery. You will notice again that I have used Mark but each of Matthew and Luke contain similar passages on the question of the challenge or confrontation that Jesus has with the established religious teachers during his period of teaching.

Whatever the accuracy or truthfulness of the above passages regarding Jesus being interviewed by the Sanhedrin and Pilate, we know that it is reported as an historical event by at least two sources outside of the New Testament that Jesus was condemned to death and was crucified. (See Chapter 5).

More recent challenges to the organised religion

In the 21st Century we would like to think that challenging the established Church or religion of a people or country would not result in someone being killed. But regrettably history and recent events in history confirm otherwise. It is said that history often repeats itself.

William Tyndale (c. 1494–1536) would agree. He was burnt at the stake for challenging the authority of the Catholic Church and for translating the Bible into English. In fact, Tyndale had not completed the translation but had drawn sufficient attention to himself as an opponent of the Catholic Church, thus, being betrayed to church officials in 1536, defrocked in an elaborate public ceremony and turned over to the civil authorities to be strangled to death and burned at the stake. His last words are said to have been, "Lord! Open the King of England's eyes".

The Tyndale Bible also challenged the Catholic Church in many other ways. The fact that it was translated into a vernacular language made it available to the common people. This allowed everyone access to scripture and gave the common people the ability to read (if they were literate) and interpret scripture how they wished, exposing it to the threat of being "twisted to their own destruction, as they do the other scriptures" (2 Peter 3:16) instead of relying on the church for their access to scripture.

The main threat that Tyndale's Bible caused to the Catholic Church is best summed up by Tyndale himself when he tells us of his reason for creating his translation in the first place. Tyndale's purpose was to **"cause a boy that driveth the plough to know more scripture than the clergy of the day"**, many of which were poorly educated. Thus Tyndale sought to undermine the Catholic Church's grip on both the access to and interpretation of scripture. The Church and its priest would no longer be needed as intercessors between the people and God.

In more recent times, the Catholic Church and other Christian churches have on at least one reasonably well known occasion excommunicated a high ranking priest.

For instance, Archbishop Le Febvre, who ironically for having insisted on saying Mass in Latin, did not acknowledge all of the changes brought about as a result of the Second Vatican Council in 1962, and ordaining four bishops against an express order not to do so.

In 1988, against the expressed prohibition of Pope John Paul II, Archbishop Le Febvre consecrated four bishops to continue his work with the Society of Saint Pius X. The Holy See immediately declared that he and the other bishops who had participated in the ceremony had incurred automatic excommunication under Catholic canon law, a status Lefebvre refused to acknowledge to his death three years later.

Le Febvre's 'crime' had nothing to do with Christian theology or the teachings of Jesus. He was excommunicated because he refused to accept the authority of the Church.

In 2009, 18 years after Lefebvre's death, Pope Benedict XVI lifted the excommunication of the four surviving bishops at their request but not to Lefebvre, therefore his excommunication remains until today.

In modern times, the threat of more violent consequences of a departure from what is perceived as the orthodox view of a religion can still be seen in so called radical clerics who purport to speak on behalf of one the world's largest religion – 'Islam' – derived from the Arabic word meaning 'listen'. It is not unknown for Islamic Cleric's to be physically attacked and/or killed for promulgating a view of the Quran or criticizing the so-called orthodox teachings.

When Jesus was teaching, human life was as cheap then as it is now.

The importance of religion and the religious leaders in what was for the Jews, their country under occupation by the Romans, should not be underestimated. The Torah and Judaism defined Jewishness and was probably the one thing that helped bond the Jews together in difficult times.

The Sanhedrin of two thousand years ago might be viewed like the Vichy Government of German occupied France in the Second World War. They co-operated with the occupiers, enjoyed privileges not shared with the rest of the population and had the ability to bring to swift justice any critics (actual or perceived) of their authority. In saying these things, I am not intending to judge either as good or bad the Vichy Government or the Sanhedrin of two thousand years ago. However, the desire to survive under occupation is understandable, though the means of survival have often been regrettable to observe.

In Kabbalah, the prophesy of a Messiah is explained in a different way. Kabbalah says that the messianic 'age' is actually the 'age of Aquarius'. Kabbalists and many spiritual teachers such as Eckhart Tolle believe that we are currently living in a time of a shift of human consciousness - at the beginning of the age of Aquarius.

This 'age' is an astrological and theological 'age'. These ages are not defined by definitive years but rather what astrologers say are shifts in the entire human consciousness. However, these ages (according to astrologers) occur approximately every two thousand years. Each age is represented as one of the twelve celestial zodiac signs. The complete cycle of the twelve ages takes in the region of twenty five thousand years.

Jesus lived during the age of Pisces – the fish. As I have previously mentioned, in Kabbalah fish are a symbolic sign of mercy and not only do fish, fishing and fishermen feature extensively throughout the Synoptic Gospels, the sign that Christians often use as a symbol of their Christianity - is the symbol of a fish.

For Kabbalists, the 'Messiah' is not an individual person appointed and anointed by God. Being created in the image and likeness of God we have each of us already been anointed. Each of us will become a messiah by attaining an appropriate level of spiritual enlightenment – by entering the kingdom. Once we do, the collective shift in consciousness will usher in the messianic age of peace, love and fellowship.

And how do we attain that spiritual enlightenment? Metaonia. A shift towards the Kingdom. As I explain in the final chapter, the Torah explains that humans were created in the image and likeness of God. Perhaps in that sense, Jesus was simply declaring what God had declared to Moses.

Metanoia – happiness is within your grasp.

Chapter 11 –
Why?

To those in search of peace and happiness it seems to me that the central message of Jesus is as relevant today as it was when he first declared it.

It is of course extremely interesting to explore the possibility and perhaps certainty that Jesus was a Kabbalist. But knowing or believing one way or the other does not of itself create happiness. Knowledge then is not sufficient. It is necessary to act on the knowledge and fulfil it. If as is possible and perhaps likely, Jesus was versed in the esoteric body of knowledge that we nowadays call 'Kabballah', it begs the question, was Jesus deeply and lastingly happy? Did what he know help him? Did he practice what he preached?

It is interesting that even if we accept that Jesus was a Kabbalist, his message was uncomplicated; short and simple to understand (like an internet meme) and in principle easy to follow.

"Metanoia, the Kingdom has drawn near."

Or put another way:

"Change the focus of your life from earthly to spiritual and you will enjoy deep and lasting happiness – NOW"

However, his message was about how to get started and take the first steps towards spiritual enlightenment. He talks about how to get to the starting point of happiness. It is by reaching at least the entry point of spiritual awareness – Malkuth (Kingdom), that you begin to feel true fulfilment and happiness. The level of happiness increases as each level of the Sephirot are reached. Malkuth (Kingdom) then is the beginning of the journey – not the end.

There is therefore an on-going need to seek to improve in spiritual awareness. That is where the 'love your neighbour as yourself' comes in. It is in our dealings with others that we can learn to reduce the influence of our ego and live in the Light – in the Kingdom.

So far as I can discern from the Synoptic Gospels, Jesus does not claim to be happy - or unhappy. If there is one thing that the Synoptic Gospels seem to lack it is any reference to happiness and humour.

But that might be because the writers of the Synoptic Gospels and those who had come into contact with Jesus just took his happy disposition and state of being for granted. They were not so much concerned with how Jesus was because to them it was obvious. Their focus was on what Jesus had to say to achieve the same elevated spiritual state – which in turn was a state of happiness anyway.

In the Synoptic Gospels, it is assumed that the route to happiness (that is to say the route from fear and unhappiness toward heaven) is desired and needed. Living under oppressive Roman occupation may have been sufficient impetus for people to seek happiness in things beyond their normal earthly day to day existence.

As we noted at the very beginning of this book, when we think about it, our greatest desire is to be deeply and lastingly happy. We noted the things that we would prefer to have if given a choice. (See Chapter 2). Well, we <u>always</u> have a choice. The core message of Jesus is that it is possible to be deeply and lastingly happy – if you choose to be. Happiness **can** be found here on earth right now (noting as before that it is only ever 'now') and it can be found by shifting our attention from the ways of the world to the Kingdom – to spiritual growth and understanding. This then, is the hidden, secret treasure – buried within you. Malkuth. The Kingdom. The Light. Deep and lasting happiness.

How might that treasure be found? 'Metanoia' – a change in direction of travel, a shift of focus and attention. The line of travel is solely towards Malkuth – the Kingdom. This is the entry point through which to achieve even higher spiritual levels of awareness and consciousness. Happiness comes from finding Malkuth - thereby being in a state of 'connection' or 'communion' with the Creator. Unhappiness is a state of un-connectedness to the Creator. It is the ways of the world. It is ego. It is the '1 per cent'.

The process is this:

1. I realise that I am unhappy.
2. I desire to be happy.
3. Happiness may only be found when connected to Malkuth, the Kingdom, the Light, the Creator.
4. How **can** I connect?
5. Metanoia.

That is it.

Well not quite. For the next step is to understand what the change of direction involves.

It is simply this.

"The first is Hear, O Israel; the Lord our God, the Lord is one; you shall love the Lord your God with all your heart, and with all your soul, and with all your mind, and with all your strength."

[Mark 12:28-30]

The total extent of the commitment to God is immediately explained in the following lines

"Keep these words that I am commanding you today in your heart. Recite them to your children and talk about them when you are at home and when you are away, when you lie down and when you rise. Bind them as a sign on your hand, fix them as an emblem on your forehead, and write them on the doorposts of your house and on your gates"

[Deuteronomy 6:6-9]

In other words: make it your number one priority. It could not be clearer. According to the Torah and therefore Judaism, Kabbalah, and Jesus, the **primary** purpose of life is to love God – the Creator.

But what does it mean to love God to this extent?

Simply put, it is an invitation to appreciate as much as we can;

- All that has been created; and
- The fact that anything has been created at all; and
- The Creator.

Appreciation and 'love' in this sense is the same as 'awe'. To fully appreciate what has been created (creation) is to be in awe of that which created it. Indeed, the universe is so remarkable it is not possible to appreciate without awe.

Nowadays there is an abundance of books and internet sites dedicated to explaining to the non-scientist the amazing complexity and size of the entire visible universe.

I invite you to read Richard Dawkins' 'The Selfish gene' and not be amazed by the intricacies and sheer genius of the human body.

Likewise, it is inspiring to read Professor Stephen Hawkings' book A Brief History of Time and marvel at the lucid way in which he describes the vastness of space and the size of the bodies found with in it.

In all instances it should be remembered that scientists have no explanation as to how the universe and all that is in it came into being in the first place – and certainly not why it has done so.

As with all things, appreciation starts with a thought – which of course is intangible. The more deeply we enter into a state of being appreciative, the more that it will become part of us. It will enter our mind, heart, body and our soul. In the end, when we totally appreciate we total assimilate. We become part of that which we appreciate.

For this increase in appreciation to happen it is necessary to bring a sense of purpose and commitment but the appreciation will actually create strength – mentally. The strength increases because the process of appreciation does two things.

1. Firstly - it shifts our attention <u>towards</u> and brings in the source of all energy – the Creator; and

2. Secondly- it shifts our attention <u>from</u> and removes all un-needed and negative things of the world.

It is a process of change, of substitution from fear to complete happiness. Ultimately, that happiness is what we call love. That is what is meant when we say that God is love. The process will create a virtuous circle.

The more we appreciate the more we are filled with appreciation and can appreciate more - and so on. For most of us, such a level of appreciation requires a significant shift in re-directing our energies from the ways of the world towards a more spiritual life of meditation, contemplation and prayer.

This does not mean becoming a religious recluse. It is a shift of priorities in our everyday lives. We cannot 'play at it'. As we have seen, the injunction in the Torah, Kabbalah and Jesus is clear. At a certain point in our lives we realise that how we are living and how we have lived does not work. It is not fulfilling.

It is like waking from a dream and realising that we have been asleep. It is like the scene in The Matrix when Neo is unplugged from his capsule or bubble. He looks around in horror as he sees that he is one of millions who are simply being used to fuel the machines.

If we are to find happiness - a change in direction is absolutely <u>necessary</u>. For some, though perhaps very few, the change or the shift can be everything and now - all at once. However, for most of us, it is a gradual process. It is of course difficult to change the momentum of a lifetime from one direction to another.

By the standards of the ordinary people at the time of Jesus, a great deal of our world is wealthy and Jesus said that it is very difficult for a wealthy person to go to heaven. But so far as we are aware, he did not say that it is impossible.

Two things must happen.

1. Firstly, the ways of the world must become unsatisfying and/or so intolerable to us (individually and collectively) that we have a strong desire to find an alternative, to change our lives and the direction of travel.

2. Secondly, we need something to re-direct our attention to and to know with certainty that whatever that is, will definitely fill the void that leaving the ways of the world creates - and feel better.

Again, it is not a question of abstinence but of substitution – with certainty. That requires an element of faith. And we have seen how important and powerful faith can be. But I hope that you noticed that I said happiness **can** be found here on earth right now.

I emphasized the word **'can'** since there is no requirement outside of us for anyone to change anything. We each of us have the free will to decide. The message is that if we are living in a state of unhappiness and we wish to find happiness, then it can be achieved but requires a change in direction towards a new target. It will not just happen of and by itself.

It is also right to say that Jesus makes it clear that if the advice is not followed then deep and lasting happiness – the Kingdom – will not be found. We will continue live on earth in the 1%, the ego dominating our every thought – with all the delusion and misery that creates.

I can hear you saying;

"But this is unfair. If God is all-powerful why did he create a world in which there is so much fear and unhappiness? Why couldn't we all just be perfect and get along anyway?"

This is a good question to ask and I will address it soon.

It has been said that:

"It is as unthinkable to conceive of the universe arising by chance without a purposeful Creator, as it is to conceive of a beautiful poem written with a random splash of ink"

(Kaplan, Handbook of Jewish Thought)

Most people think of Albert Einstein as a physicist who 'invented' the General Theory of Relativity, the famous equation $E = mc^2$ and several other related theories.

In 1921 he was awarded the Nobel Prize in Physics for his work in theoretical physics. His discovery of the law of the photoelectric effect was a pivotal step in the evolution of quantum theory.

But what is generally not appreciated about Einstein is that he was a very philosophical and spiritual man. Einstein accepted that there is a creator of the universe and he referred to the creator as God. Einstein appreciated with humility, awe and wonder the complexity of the Universe and saw his work as a means to understand creation and the Creator.

Here are some examples of things that Einstein is quoted as saying:

"One cannot help but be in awe when he contemplates the mysteries of eternity, of life, of the marvellous structure of reality. It is enough if one tries merely to comprehend a little of this mystery each day"

"There are only two ways to live your life. One is as though nothing is a miracle. The other is as though everything is a miracle"

"Joy in looking and comprehending is nature's most beautiful gift."

"Science without religion is lame, religion without science is blind."

Of course most people have also heard of the Physicist Professor Stephen Hawking. In his earlier years he seemed to profess a dismissive and disdainful attitude towards the concept of there being a Creator or God. But over time his attitude appears to have shifted. He too echoes the sense of awe and wonder concerning the Universe. Again, here are some selected quotations:

"The whole history of science has been the gradual realisation that events do not happen in an arbitrary manner, but that they reflect a certain underlying order, which may or may not be divinely inspired."

"Look up at the stars and not down at your feet. Try to make sense of what you see, and wonder about what makes the universe exist. Be curious."

"I want to know why the universe exists, why there is something greater than nothing."

In the context of what we have been looking at in this book, it is apparent that it is not necessary to be a 'religious person' to contemplate and appreciate the universe and to do so with awe and wonder.

Both Einstein and Hawking in their slightly different ways 'appreciate' creation and the very fact of creation. In doing so, whether they realise it or not (and in the case of Einstein I think he did), they are appreciating the Creator. It is fair to point out that Stephen Hawking does not entirely discount the possibility of there being a Creator.

There are two main areas of enquiry or disciplines within the science of theoretical physics. One deals with the laws of physics on the very large scale (Astrophysics) and the other with the laws of physics on the very small scale (Quantum Physics). The first deals with the stars, planets, black holes, galaxies and the like. The latter with atoms, electrons, quarks. In short, energy on the large scale (Macro) and energy on the small (Micro) scale.

But the laws of physics that govern things on the large scale are not the same as those on the small scale – and vice versa. The respective laws break down and do not work once applied to the other.

It has been the quest of physicists including Einstein and Hawking (and many, many others) to find a theory of physics that unites the two. It is the Holy Grail of physics. But as Stephen Hawking remarks in his book the **Illustrated Brief History of Time**:

"Even if there is only one possible unified theory it is just a set of rules and equations. What is it that breathes fire into the equations and makes a universe for them to describe? The usual approach of science of constructing a mathematical model cannot answer the question of why there should be a universe for the model to describe."

"Why does the Universe go to all the bother of existing?"

He concedes that he does not have the answer. Up to now he says;

"most scientists have been too occupied with the development of new theories that describe what the universe is to ask the question why."

Before becoming a Rabbi and renowned scholar, Rabbi Aryeh Kaplan was a physicist, the youngest physicist to be employed by the United States government.

In his book '**A handbook of Jewish thought**', he explains that Judaism considers that both man and nature were created by a purposeful being 'God'.

He explains that it is argued from a mathematical point of view that;

"the more complex an ordered structure, the less, the probability of its structure being due to chance. The chemistry of life is by far the most complex process in our experience, and yet we find that the inorganic matter of the universe supports the process. Since there is only one type of matter in the universe, the chances of its having all the chemical and physical properties needed to support life are remotely small, unless we take into account a purposeful Creator. In essence, it is the properties of the electron that make possible the existence of the human brain."
But 'who' you may ask, created the electron?

- Indeed, 'who' created the properties of the electron?
- In fact, 'who' conceived of the properties?

- Moreover, 'who' created the 'thing' that created the properties of the electron.
- And finally, who conceived of the 'who', 'person', 'thing' that conceived of all of these things?

The answer of course is the uncaused cause, God. But as Stephen Hawking asks - why does the universe exist? Or put another way, why did God create the universe, you and me - everything?

The 'why' element is a mystery. It is however, true that Judaism and Kabbalah and for that matter Christianity suggest that God made humans in his image and likeness. But the Torah says more than that.

In his book 'The Living Torah (A new Translation based on traditional Jewish sources), Rabbi Aryeh Kaplan translates Bereshith 1:26-27 (Genesis) as follows:

"God said, ''<u>Let us make man with our image and likeness</u>. Let him dominate the fish of the sea, the birds of the sky, the livestock of animals, and all the earth – and every land animal that walks the earth. God [thus] created man with His image. In the image of God, He created them, male and female He created them.''

[Kaplan]

The New Revised Standard Version of the same passage is as follows:

"Then God said, let us make humankind in our image, according to our likeness; and let them have dominion over the fish of the sea, and over the birds of the air, and over the cattle, and over all the wild animals of the earth, and over creeping thing that creeps upon the earth. So God created humankind in his image, in the image of God he created them; male and female he created them."

[Genesis 1:26-27]

According to Rabbi Kaplan's translation God thus created man <u>with</u> his image. <u>In</u> the image of God, he created him, male and female. He created them'

[My emphasis].

God then has both male and female aspects. But notice the distinction that the words **with** and **in** imply.

"with his image" could mean either:

- Man had built into him what God has – here 'with' means 'includes' or 'in his image'; or
- It was the image that created man – here 'with' means 'by' or 'using his image'.

This passage from Genesis seeks to explain the origins of the world in which we live but it does not explain 'why' humans and the universe were created and is kept in being.

What this seems to be saying is that humans were created by God and we have the same ability to create. The image and likeness would include the ability to create. We have even seen in the Sefer Yetzirah that it is considered possible for a highly spiritual person to create from nothing – exercise control over nature and actually to create a being – a Golem. (See Chapter 4).

But the question that is not answered is 'why'? As Stephen Hawking says:

'Why does the Universe go to all the bother of existing?'

Why did God create the universe, including you and me?

In his book, **Conversations with God - Book 1,** Neale Donald Walsh says that in his conversations with God, God tells him that God created humans and all that is because he wanted to 'experience' things for himself. God knew himself. He knew what existence is and no existence is. But he wanted to experience it. He could only experience it by creating.

Neal says that God told him:

'My purpose in creating you, my Spiritual offspring, was for me to know Myself as God.'

The logical inference being that God could not know himself as the Creator unless and until he had actually created. Another word for creation might be 'manifestation'. It is not possible to have manifestation unless what is manifested is perceived.

The creation of conscious beings is the creation of something that holds up a mirror to that which has been created – and therefore the Creator. This I think is what Bereshith and Genesis (above mentioned) is referring to in talking of humankind being created by and in the image of the Creator.

Until creation, creation was only a potential and the Creator as Creator was only a potential. The act of creation reflected God and in the process he created that which could create.

We have already seen that it is part of the belief system of Kabbalah and Judaism that humans are created with and in the image and likeness of God. One of God's abilities is to create. The desire and the ability to create is an important feature of Kabbalah but it is not the only God like trait that we possess.

In his book the Power of Kabbalah, Yehudi Berg says:

'When we look into the reality of the 99 Percent, we discover four key attributes of the Light that we inherited and need to express in our world...They are:

- **Being the cause**
- **Being a creator**
- **Being in control**
- **Sharing'**

The extent to which we can be the cause, create, be in control and share is reflective of our spiritual level of consciousness. The closer to God, the source of all things – the greater the power to do all of these things.

But remember also, before creation, God was not physical. He simply was. He was potential. If it is correct that we are created in the image and likeness of God, then we too are potential. We too are eternal. We too are infinite.

When we 'connect' to 'Malkuth', the Ten Sephirot, God, or the Light – when we let go, surrender to what 'is' and become present in the 'now', we are at the first run of the ladder to remembering and realising these other aspects of who we are. Each cell of a human embryo is separate and distinct. It has a particular function. But each and every one of the trillion cells carries with it the blueprint for every other cell and every other part of the human body.

Is it not possible therefore that this is our experience with creation and the Creator as a whole? We are each of us unique manifestations of the creator and yet we carry within us all of creation.

But ultimately, in our human form as physical beings we cannot 'know' the essence of the creator. We cannot 'understand' God. God is unknowable. God is a mystery. At best, we can 'sense' our connection to our source of being and we can become ever more aware of that source.

In the same we that we can experience light at ever-greater intensity as we draw closer to it. This is the process that is described in the Ten Sephirot. Our awareness is developed by appreciation. We have come full circle. We are back to appreciating God.

Finally, I will deal with the question of why it is that God did not create a perfect world.

In Kabbalah, there is a concept of what is called 'the bread of shame'. We cannot experience true happiness without having to face challenges. Anything of value is only of value if we appreciate it, and we best appreciate things that we have earned rather than been given. If God had simply created a world in which we were all perfect, where would be the merit and joy in doing the right thing?

Often the challenges we face involve choices. We have been given free will to choose to do the right thing or the wrong thing. Our merit and enjoyment of life is derived from the choices we make and acting on them.

Assuming we could do so (and many parents can), if we simply gave our children whatever they asked for without their having 'earned it', their sense of self-worth and value would not exist. What we are denying our children when we simply give them everything, is the opportunity to create. They are being denied the opportunity to earn their bread and to appreciate the outcome of their efforts. That is shameful of us as givers and to them as receivers. That is the bread of shame.

It is for this reason that God did not create a perfect world. He created the potential for a perfect world. He wanted us to work for it. In that way we would properly appreciate it.

We read in The Living Torah:

"God saw that man's wickedness on earth was increasing. Every impulse of his innermost thought was only for evil, all day long. God regretted that He had made man on earth, and he was pained to His very core. God said, ''I will obliterate humanity that I have created from the face of the earth...I regret that I created them''. But Noah found favour in God's eyes."

[Bereshith 6:5-8] – see also Genesis 6:5-7.

God did not create an imperfect world. He did not create an evil world. But it seems to me that it is true to say that God did create a world in which both good and evil might exist. In this sense, God created both good and evil. If the Torah is accepted, that must be right.

The Tree of Knowledge and of Good and Evil cannot be of relevance without good and evil. God created the opportunity for us to create a perfect world – a world of good without evil. Likewise, he created the opportunity for us to create an imperfect world that might include evil. Evil in our world is not of God's making – it is of our making.

But note, when we talk of good and evil, we are talking from the perspective of the one percent (1%), from the ego. Good and evil only arise from knowledge of what is good and evil which is restricted in and by the world of time and space – and that is not the Tree of Life.

In the Tree of Life, each state of consciousness takes us away from making judgments and into the spiritual worlds of no judgment and just 'being' in communion with our other attributes – eternal and infinite. We could not know what a perfect world is without knowing what an imperfect world is. When ultimately, we create a perfect world, it will be because we have made the effort and will enjoy the fruits of our efforts (singular and collectively) all the more.

God created the same opportunity for us. We have the same opportunity to create and that is why we exist. We have a choice. We exercise that choice every second of every minute of every hour of every day. We have been doing so for a long time.

Many of us have come to fully understand that there is a choice, that we can make it if we choose to obtain real happiness. Unfortunately, so far, insufficient number of us have either not chosen or made the wrong choice.

But that position too is changing and at some juncture there will be tipping point. When that happens, more people will choose to move towards a higher Consciousness - the Kingdom - than those who do not and the momentum of the consciousness of the world will also experience metanoia and connect to the Kingdom en masse.

You can choose to add to the number who choose metanoia and in the process cause, create, control and share your experience and outcome with all you meet. You will add to the momentum both directly and indirectly.

Every human being has the potential to create. It involves one simple thing:

Love your neighbour

In every circumstance that you find yourself involving your dealings with other human beings there are two things you should do:

1. Pause for thought. Before speaking or acting (or not speaking or not acting) wait until any anger, frustration, passion, excitement has passed; then
2. Ask yourself this question:

'How would I wish to be treated if I were the other person?'

As you proceed through life aware of your response to the 'challenges' you face and as you incorporate 'love your neighbour' into all your dealings, you will enter and remain in the Kingdom and move ever higher through the spiritual levels of the Ten Sephirot.

It is in this process that you will find true, deep and lasting happiness.

I wish you joy and every blessing on your journey.

Metanoia – heaven is within your grasp. Metanoia – true happiness is yours for the taking.

Paul A Westerman
London
2017

22029993R00167

Printed in Great Britain
by Amazon